Endorsem~

"There is a powerful purpose inside every one of focused, can make any vision a reality. This book ca~ ... ~.~uuctive force with wisdom and real-world common sense."

Richard Leider
Bestselling author of *Repacking Your Bags* & *The Power of Purpose*

"In today's world of fast paced, gen "Y", hi tech, global, multi-tasked, "matrixed", productivity crazed, speed to win world, it is refreshing to read a book that focuses on the whole person. It makes a ton of sense to take time to understand what really matters in life and in business before charging ahead into the uncertain future we all share."

Bill Reina
Procter and Gamble / Director / Global Talent Group

"Get this book…it's both practical and revealing at the executive, operational and personal levels. Bud Roth provides a strong step-wise progression through the somewhat confusing picture of how to engage and be successful in today's organizations. He presents a wealth of useful tools, exercises and informational summaries written in a clear, concise, engaging and coherent fashion. Buy it—it can make a difference in your career and life."

Charles H. Bishop, Jr., Ph.D.
Author, *Making Change Happen One Person at a Time*, Consultant to Executive Teams: ADT, Quaker Oats, Baxter Healthcare

"Have you reached your full potential yet? If not…read Bud Roth's book and learn how to elevate your effectiveness by harnessing the personal energy from clarity of purpose & prioritization of values. Get ready to accelerate your growth & change. You can "will" it."

Robert (Bob) Grimm, Ed.D.
Professor, Kelley School of Business, Indiana University

"What I loved about Bud Roth's book is that it helped me switch my focus of living based on *Tasks* to the *Process* of living. If we get wrapped up in what we need to get done, we can lose the essence of our life "in process." The questions: At what cost?", "Do I really enjoy what I'm doing?" "What does it all count for?" "Is this the life and work I'm enjoying or just putting off?" have awakened me to a critical view of what is truly more productive and life enhancing. Thanks, Bud!"

Hayden D.M. Hayden
CEO of Enlightened-Leaders
Master Facilitator of Crucial Conversations®, Vital Smarts

Be More Productive— Slow Down

Design the Life and Work You Want

Bud Roth

iUniverse LLC
Bloomington

Be More Productive— Slow Down
Design the Life and Work You Want

iUniverse books may be ordered through booksellers or by contacting:

iUniverse LLC
1663 Liberty Drive
Bloomington, IN 47403
www.iuniverse.com
1-800-Authors (1-800-288-4677)

Because of the dynamic nature of the Internet, any web addresses or links contained in this book may have changed since publication and may no longer be valid. The views expressed in this work are solely those of the author and do not necessarily reflect the views of the publisher, and the publisher hereby disclaims any responsibility for them.

Any people depicted in stock imagery provided by Thinkstock are models, and such images are being used for illustrative purposes only.

Certain stock imagery © Thinkstock.

ISBN: 978-1-4620-1872-7 (sc)
ISBN: 978-1-4620-1873-4 (hc)
ISBN: 978-1-4620-1874-1 (ebk)

Printed in the United States of America

iUniverse rev. date: 06/26/2013

For my wife, Cathy

Contents

Part IV
Maintaining Purpose and Progress

Acknowledgments

I must first thank my wife, Cathy, for inspiring me to persist and complete the book and then to "get the book published!" I am deeply grateful for her help with the necessary details of this project, as well as providing a critical eye.

My son David designed the cover and the models for the book, as well as providing encouragement and ideas throughout the process.

Daughters Cindy and Amy provided continuous encouragement. Amy appropriately challenged my approach to helping my audience sustain the learning experience; thus "Time to Pause." She also provided helpful resources.

Deb Buehler, writing coach, was very good at gently suggesting changes that I took very seriously. I appreciated her encouragement and her way of keeping me on task.

I appreciated the time that my colleagues spent reading the copy and providing their endorsements.

I need to also thank other family members and close friends for their encouragement, research materials, and stories, which may, *or may not*, be included in these pages.

It is my sincere hope that my family, grandchildren, and friends can find enlightenment for their lives among these pages.

Introduction

I: We hear it all the time. "We/I need to make some changes." Or, "The only thing that's constant is change." Change is the central reality of our time. Individuals, as well as large organizations, must manage immense amounts of ongoing change at all levels.

I want to help you experience long-term joy in your life. It's difficult for most people to slow down enough to confront the way they currently live and then to make choices that change or enhance the way they are living and working. I want to give you the tools to renew yourself when change is thrust upon you or when you realize that "I/we need to make some changes."

How do we create and manage the changes in our lives? We need to learn to live and work in cycles of changes. For individuals, this means gaining the necessary entrepreneurial capabilities to effectively manage themselves throughout the many disruptions in life.

It is critical for individuals to:

1. Be aware of who you are and what you really want to do

2. Take control of your situation

3. Stay grounded in your values and principles

4. Become stable by controlling what you can control

5. Plan your future and execute the plan

6. Renew yourself and your plans when change confronts you

In businesses, this means keeping in step with technological changes, as well as dealing in the global marketplace.

It's critical for any business or enterprise to:

1. Accelerate the development of the organization

2. Focus on the mission at hand and not get misdirected

3. Continuously enhance leadership effectiveness

4. Ensure that all employees are deeply engaged in order to allow creativity and self-management

5. Continuously improve performance to a higher level

6. Increase the effectiveness of handling change

7. Renew the organization's purpose and mission frequently: at least once each year

II: After more than thirty years doing corporate, consulting, and coaching work, I noticed that many people continue to have difficulty living satisfying lives, and I wanted to reach a larger audience. I wanted to help people realize that they can *design* the life they want to lead.

How do I know about the pain and joy that people go through? I'm a husband, father, and grandfather (Papa!) first and foremost. I worked in seven large corporations in sales and training and spent twenty-three years in human resources. I've worked in manufacturing, financial services, marketing, distribution, and information services. I've also worked outside of the United States in Singapore as the human resource manager for the Far East region. I've worked in roles ranging from an individual contributor role to a vice president. I've been an entrepreneur for the last thirteen years, leveraging my past experience to help people by listening to their experiences, issues, and desires. Then I help them plan their life and take action to move forward, change direction, and grow. I show people how to change their lives in order to get what they want for themselves and their families. I help people accelerate changes that they want while staying in control of what they can control.

Many executive and middle managers I coached didn't know that more was in their control than they thought. When they became aware of their behavior, they changed the approach and behavior of their leadership style. They gained more influence over the results and accelerated projects to completion, with better outcomes. They learned to manage relationships, plan their projects, and execute their business more effectively after they realized that they influenced others by collaborating with, listening to, and learning from the people they lead.

It's as important to be productive in our personal and family lives, as well as our work. I help executives to balance the professional side with the personal side. They learned that they can have a more satisfying life when they are the same person at home as they are at work. Individual coaching is very personal. It is also more effective when personal and work lives are integrated. This is the reason I discuss both sides of life in this book. In my organizational development consulting role, I use Group Coaching to establish productive cooperation *across* functional divisions. Group coaching establishes a safe environment for leaders to learn more about each other and build trust, interdependent awareness, and the willingness to help each other in a variety of ways. Leaders learn that the organization is more productive when they align their collective projects and activities with the mission of the business. They experience the power of sharing information across the organization and enabling employees to do what they do best. The tag line for my business is *Sharing Knowledge is Powerful*.

III: If you are between the ages of twenty and one hundred and are looking for a way to move your life or work to the next level, then you will want to read this book. If you are looking to reinvent yourself, you will be excited by the prospect of taking actions that can change your life. You will benefit whether you are a parent or single, a doctor, manager, executive, corporate worker, entrepreneur, knowledge worker, or someone who wants more joy in your life.

How to read this book

At the end of each chapter, you will find questions and advice meant to help you achieve what you really want in your personal *and* professional life. I don't believe you can live a satisfying life by separating who you are and how you behave in either environment. The exercises are also condensed in the Appendix.

It will be helpful to have a journaling booklet handy for you to record your thoughts and ideas, as well as respond to the questions at the back of each chapter. You may want to look at the exercises and questions before you start reading the chapter in order to highlight important topics as you read.

I suggest that you download the free workbook before you start reading. You will find the workbook on the website under "Resources", Go to bemoreproductive-slowdown.com. The workbook has additional reflective questions and exercises that are very beneficial. The workbook *slows you down* to become more aware of yourself, discover what is important and take action. We want to you to live your life and work the way you design it to unfold.

How you live your life and perform your work is very important to you. I suggest that you contemplate my ideas as they apply to you in order to design a good plan. Most people want to lead both their personal and professional lives productively, effectively, and enthusiastically. I want you to slow down in order to help you get further ahead and actually accelerate living a successful life.

You can read this book during a ride at jet speed from New York to Denver, but you won't be able to apply my guidance. My hope is that you reflect on every chapter—and at times a single paragraph—that stimulates fresh thoughts in your heart and mind. Slow down to perform the exercises before you.

While going through the exercises, you may want to form a group of friends or colleagues to share thoughts and experiences and collaborate. This group interaction may help you make better choices for yourself.

It is my hope that by the end of this book you will experience the power you have to change your life by:

- Learning how to slow down and experience the benefits
- Being more productive in your personal and business lives
- Learning how to take control of the way you want to live your life, as well as your work environment
- Creating a simple, written plan for the way you want to live
- Renewing the passion in your life and work
- Learning about how you can take care of yourself, your family, and your work while living the life that you've designed

Please continue your learning and sharing your knowledge with me through blog posts at bemoreproductive-slowdown.com.

Don't forget a notebook for capturing your thoughts and writing your plan as you design your life and work.

Bud Roth
Carmel, Indiana

Part I:
Living Life Out of Control

1
The Fast-Changing World: Living Without Purpose

The times we live in are moving at a faster rate every year, and we can get caught up in these busy times. It is crucial for us to respond to the fast-changing environment by planning our life, knowing that these conditions will continue.

Picture the Goals

What does it take to meet your goals? We will briefly look at the professional side of setting meeting a goal and then the personal side. A leader needs to keep people in the company focused on the outcomes of the annual strategy or mission. First, it's important for you to know why you are doing certain work. Leaders must then help you stay focused; not only on why and where you are going, but also on how you execute the work. Usually you are left on your own to do the work. Good leaders continuously remind others of the purpose and direction. It's your role to figure out how to fulfill the mission with the help of others through cooperation and collaboration. Leaders must create *pictures* of the outcomes or goals of the organization. You may have seen such pictures on the office walls. Some corporations have spent over one million dollars to print and post illustrations of the journey of the mission on the interior walls of the buildings. They want the mission understood in simple terms, pictured in your mind. It works.

Why shouldn't you do this for your personal life? Pictures of your future plans and desires help you navigate the journey. Pictures keep you on track and help you maintain momentum as you move toward your goals. Integrating your personal and professional purposes is important to creating appropriate balance and control in your life. It's easy to let business or work control your personal life. It's easy to lose perspective of what is right for you or even what may be right for the business. Fooling yourself into thinking that your work life is the more important because it facilitates survival can warp your perspective. This misconception can also take you in a direction that throws you off of where you really want to go. You can become a workaholic, working yourself so hard that it impacts family life.

Busyness, Multitasking, and Overcommitting

Work is where we usually relate to productivity and speed, since we are measured by these elements. Let's look at the work environment to understand the importance of purpose, planning, and slowing down. Speed and simply accomplishing tasks may be busyness that satisfies the desire to check things off our "To Do" list. However, priorities must drive activities in the work environment. If you aren't working on meaningful activities, you may be wasting your time. Working too fast may also affect the quality of work you do. The quality of the work will definitely impact the desired outcomes.

Busyness, multitasking, and overcommitting are habits that reduce effectiveness and decrease genuine productivity. Busyness is when we are busy doing tasks that are not significant and are not focused on our mission or purpose. For example: I can be busy checking my e-mail frequently throughout the day, researching information on the Internet and making phone calls to follow up on volunteer activities. "It was important for me today to call prospective clients and follow up on referrals, but I just couldn't get to it." This is how I rationalize wasting time.

Interruptions frequently add to busyness and disrupt concentration and focus. These uncontrollable events can affect our productivity and the quality of the outcomes. A *New York Times* article pointed to a research project at the Institute for the Future of the Mind at Oxford University.[1] It suggests that the popular perception of multitasking is open to question. A group of eighteen- to twenty-one-year-olds and a group of thirty-five- to thirty-nine-year-olds were both given ninety seconds to translate images into numbers, using a simple code. The younger group did 10 percent better when not interrupted. But when both groups were interrupted by a phone call, a cell phone short-text message, or an instant message, the older group matched the younger group in speed and accuracy. "The older people think more slowly, but they have a faster fluid intelligence, so they are better able to block out interruptions and choose what to focus on," said Martin Westwell, thirty-six, deputy director of the institute. Westwell has changed his work habits since completing the research project.

Completely focusing on the task at hand, without interruptions, generates speedy conclusions, as well as good results. By the same token, focusing on speed, trying to think about too many things at a time, and allowing interruptions can slow down the process and negatively affect results. Multitasking can be harmful to an individual or group of workers. It is usually stressful to think about so many things at one time. Leave the multitasking to the computers, machines, and robots. We humans were not made for multitasking. We can only think about one thing at a time.

Interruptions frequently come in the form of switching tasks. In choosing to multitask, you may be choosing your own level of interruptions, less productive work, and mediocre quality.

In 1984, Tom DeMarco, author of *Slack*,[2] and his colleague at the Atlantic Systems Guild began a three-year study of software developers titled "Programmer Performance and the Effects of the Workplace."

"We collected information about the environment and recorded each and every task switch. To no one's surprise, people who were interrupted less often performed better. We modeled performance against task-switching frequency and came to the conclusion that the best way to understand task switching was to assume that each switch imposes a direct penalty of a bit more than twenty minutes of lost concentration. We also noted an average

1   Lohr, Steve, "Slow Down Brave Multitasker and Don't Read This in Traffic," *New York Times*, quoting Institute for the Future of the Mind at Oxford University, March 26, 2007.

2   DeMarco, Tom, *Slack: Getting Past Burnout, Busywork, and the Myth of Total Efficiency*, Broadway Books, New York, 2001.

of nearly 0.4 switches per hour. This result is a direct loss of productive effort of more than one hour per day," reported DeMarco. "Fragmented knowledge workers may look busy, but a lot of their busyness is just thrashing, switching continually from one activity to another."

Perhaps pressures surround you, forcing you in many directions and constantly changing the priorities in your life and work. The pace of change alone can increase pressure. If pressure gets out of control, you are not going to accomplish what you really want to achieve. This means that you will be less productive in accomplishing the top priorities. You can become overcommitted under pressure to do more and may find yourself multitasking to keep up. "Do more!" "Just get it done!" On and on it goes, until you are out of control, along with others working with you.

An example of being overcommitted and out of control in the work environment is when workers are let go for whatever reason and you must then do two jobs or part of another person's work. Now you have fifteen top-priority tasks or projects versus the ten you previously performed. Expectations increase, along with more interactions, meetings, deadlines, research, communicating, changes, reordering priorities, etc. You are expected to adapt and get the work done. Shifting from task to task or project to project demands greater organization, discipline, and just hard work at a faster pace. This frequent shifting creates additional stress and generates multitasking, potential errors, and usually poorer outcomes than you'd like.

An example of overcommitment on a personal front may be when the mother of three children under seven years old, one in school full-time, one in school half days, one in diapers at two years old, has overloaded her days. This typical scenario may be familiar.

- Volunteers to organize a book sale festival
- Volunteers for Wednesday's church activities
- Plays tennis once a week
- Works out four times a week
- Cleans her own house
- Goes to T-ball games with the five-year-old on Thursdays

- Attends soccer practice for the seven-year-old plus a game on Saturdays
- Plans the menu and prepares the meals
- Helps the seven-year-old with studies
- Makes sure the two-year-old meets with other kids each week
- Plans a camping trip for the next weekend with friends
- Goes to the doctor for bad colds, ear aches, etc.
- Maintains the car, including oil changes and repairs
- Plans for guests visiting in three weeks
- Plans and holds birthday parties and attends those of friends
- Sometimes talks to her husband

You can probably think of more events and activities to add to *your* list.

We may say that this is just "life." But this mother must multitask to get through the day and week. She lives with a high level of stress. She is also concerned about the quality time she has for each child and her husband, not to mention time for herself. She is exhausted each night by 7:00, preparing for the next day as she folds the laundry. This mom is overcommitted and may be out of control.

I can only think of one or two justifiable situations for multitasking. My daughter has three boys under the age of six. She says that the family can't survive unless she multitasks. I worry about the pressure on moms like her. I understand they do the things they need to do. I know that the millennial generation is proud of the way they can multitask, but I believe it impacts quality of life, inhibits clear thinking, and disrupts the focus on the highest priorities.

The "Why Home School" blog refers to a Time.com article[3] called "The Multitasking Generation" that focuses on how children of this generation do a lot of multitasking and some of the problems resulting from constant multitasking. "Decades of research indicate that the quality

---

3   The Multitasking Generation blog, "Why Homework?" Time.com.

of one's output and depth of thought deteriorated as one attends to ever more tasks. Research shows that our brains don't do true multitasking. We can not give full attention to a conversation while typing an e-mail to another friend about a different topic, while focusing on something else in the background. Habitual multitasking may condition their brain to an overexcited state, making it difficult to focus even when they want to. People lose the skill and the will to maintain concentration …"

Paul Pearsall, PhD, wrote in *Toxic Success*,[4] "Anyone who brags of being a multitasker is confessing to being a sufferer of toxic success syndrome. Research indicates that multitasking is another name for attention deficit disorder and lack of productivity and effectiveness."

The article, "Drop that BlackBerry! Multitasking may be harmful," on CNNhealth.com[5], described the impact of multitasking based on a study by the Proceedings of the National Academy of Sciences. "A new study suggests that people who often do multiple tasks in a variety of media— texting, instant messaging, online video watching, work processing, web surfing, and more—do worse on tests in which they need to switch attention from one task to another than people who rarely multitask in this way." The article also mentioned that "This study adds to a growing body of literature that says, in general, that multitasking is going to be problematic for people, that it does compromise productivity, and that its consequences can be quite severe in situations like driving." says David W. Goodman, MD, the director of the Adult Attention Deficit Disorder Center of Maryland.

Indeed, we all hear more news coverage these days about auto accidents linked to texting, making phone calls, and reading e-mails on smart phones while driving. Multitasking can literally lead to death. But we are mostly concerned with the stress, pressure, low productivity, interruptions, and lack of focus when multitasking. These conditions negatively impact our quality of life and impede our enjoyment of satisfying work.

Without these stressful conditions, you have better quality time, the tasks are completed faster, and you can move on to another priority.

---

4   Pearsall, Paul, PhD, *Toxic Success, How to Stop Striving and Start Thriving*, Ocean Publishing, Inc., 2002

5   "Drop that BlackBerry! Multitasking may be harmful." *Health Magazine*, 2009, http://www.cnn.com/2009/HEALTH/08/25/multitasking.harmful/index.html.

Get tasks off your mind and move on: complete them. Use contiguous thinking to concentrate on the outcomes without straying to other topics and thoughts. Focus on the details as you progress toward completion. Concentration allows you to think about the impact and other important elements within the task. You don't risk losing the thoughts that will enhance the project or task.

Chronic Multitasking

The following research proves that multitasking can actually impair brain functioning. "If this sounds more like an affliction than a resume booster, that's because research has shown again and again that the human mind isn't meant to multitask Even worse, research show that multitasking can have long-term, harmful effects on brain function.

In a 2009 study, Stanford researcher, Clifford Nass, challenged 262 students to complete experiments that involved switching among tasks, filtering irrelevant information, and using working memory. Nass and his colleagues expected that frequent multitaskers would outperform non-multitaskers on at least some of these activities.

They found the opposite: Chronic multitaskers were abysmal at all three tasks. The scariest part; Only one of the experiments actually involved multitasking, signaling to Nass that even when they focus on a single activity, frequent multitaskers use their brains less effectively.

Multitasking is a weakness, not strength. In 2010, a study by neuroscientists at the French medical research agency, INSERM, showed that when people focus on two tasks simultaneously, each side of the brain tackles a different task.

This suggests a two-task limit on what the human brain can handle. Taking on more tasks increases the likelihood of errors, so Nass suggests what he calls the 20-minute rule. Rather than switching tasks from minute to minute, dedicate a 20-minute chunk of time to a single task, then switch to the next one."[6]

---

6   "Don't Multitask—Your Brain Will Thank You", "Get More Done", Issie Lapowsky, Inc., April, 2013, page 66

Disconnected Tasks

"Shotgunning," or distributing your energy over a wide variety of tasks, may dilute your effectiveness the same way as interruptions do. You may have more control over the approach to your work because you can make the choice of "rifle shooting" on one task before you move on to another priority or "shotgunning" on many tasks. By focusing your concentration, you screen out thoughts and tasks that take you away from your mission. Take control over how you work, even within a potentially disruptive work environment. Sometimes you need to just say no, with an appropriate explanation, to some requests. Find a good place to work when completing critical projects with deadlines; change the location where you are working in order to concentrate and maintain focus. Cover your movements with your boss if necessary, but take action.

If your actions are not consistent with the culture or your manager's expectations, something is out of synch and needs to be addressed. Experiment with doing the work a different way to improve your productivity. Have a conversation with your manager to let her know what you are doing and why. This action can be considered healthy "pushback." It is useful in improving how tasks are accomplished to meet the desired outcomes. Share what you've learned with your manager and coworkers.

You experience the satisfaction of doing good work instead of doing many disconnected tasks. The disconnected tasks are busyness. You may try to get the tasks done very quickly in order to check them off. You may allow frequent interruptions, such as reading an incoming e-mail when the digital tone sounds, answering calls, and answering e-mails as they arrive throughout the day. You are stressing yourself out while fooling yourself that you are productive because you are busy.

Focused concentration is powerful and very productive. Don't allow the environment to become disruptive to the point of not being able to control it.

- Turn off the tone sound for incoming e-mail

- Place your phone on "forward to voice mail"

- Silence your mobile phone, Droid, iPhone, Blackberry, or other devices.

Fear Factor

Fear can be one of the reasons we multitask. I'm talking from personal experience. We do many things at once because someone told us to do it. We don't want to lose our job; we don't want a mediocre or poor performance rating; and on and on. Another reason may be because we live with the illusion that we are heroes if we multitask: it's a badge of honor. These heroic misconceptions are not the most productive modes of operation. The "heroics" become habit-forming and even addictive. We are running downhill at breakneck speed and don't know how to slow or stop ourselves. And we don't realize that we are doing this out of fear.

Business is Business

Corporations rarely, if ever, suggest slowing down to be more productive. "Do more with less" is the current mantra of many businesses. For the most part, corporate environments contradict many of the concepts I discuss in these chapters. At times, corporate direction seems to be focused more on quantity and speed than quality. Leaders frequently overcommit to get more work out of the workforce. Then the quality may be impacted because of the expected speed of delivery. Of course, our customers can be very demanding about delivery requests, but pushing for more output, more responsibilities, and more projects forces multitasking. This seems to be the mode of operation for most businesses. And with every leadership change and reorganization, things seem to get worse for the managers and individual workers, not better. Leaders want us to get more done and reduce costs. "Work smarter" really means "bust your buns," "work longer hours," and "just make it happen."

Let's not leave out the small company or even the solo entrepreneur. We think we can do everything and keep bringing in more business. The passion of small businesses frequently ignores limited capacity and quality of delivery for quantity of numbers. As small as a business may be, we can get stuck focusing on just getting more of the same clients or selling more of the same products or services. This leads to stress, and multitasking is required. We frequently don't slow down to consider other creative approaches to the business we are in. We also don't ask for help from others. We stick with what we've always known or have done successfully in the past. This is how we become overcommitted and overwhelmed and start the downward spiral.

Determine Your Purpose

Many of us let too much get in the way of the real priorities. Desired outcomes can be elusive if you don't focus on your purpose for why you are doing something. You will get further faster if you live your life with intention; that is, knowing specifically what you want in your life and work and taking the actions that will get you there. Achieving your mission is very satisfying because it fulfills a purpose.

Spending time thinking about *why* you are doing what you are doing may get you where you want to go more quickly. If you are fulfilling someone else's request, make sure you understand *their* purpose and how this fits in with the overall intent and strategy. You may need to ask clarifying questions of yourself, your boss, or colleagues to see a clear purpose in your own mind. We can all do a better job if we clearly understand what's expected and why. It may take some courage to ask questions for clarity, but taking the initiative to clearly understand, particularly if you are being held accountable, will be worth it. Purpose is clearly established by making sure you understand why you are taking this action(s). Then develop a plan to accomplish the task. Finally, execute the plan.

Clear Your Head

If you find yourself in such chaos, slow down, clear your head, and refocus on what is *really* important for you to be working on. You may be a CEO, C-level executive, middle manager, or individual contributor. These concepts and thought-provoking pauses are important at all levels of the organization.

An independent group of very successful consultants and executive coaches is attached to my organization. I need to clearly understand the purpose of each individual, as well as the purpose of us working together. My colleagues push back on suggestions that come from any one of us if they aren't clear about what we want to accomplish. Our activities must make sense and have purpose. No one can afford to spend much time dancing around a misunderstood purpose. Each one wants to help accomplish the activity in some way, as long as we are clear about our objectives. That's great synergy. We don't waste our time or energy, but we do take time to clear up any doubts about where we are going and why. Frequently ask yourself:

- Why am I doing this?
- Is this task necessary or important?
- Is this my highest priority?
- Is there something I don't see about this task that I may be missing?
- Am I allowing something into my day or time that isn't going to help meet my objectives?

These and other questions help center us to maintain productive activity levels. Moving ahead in the right direction isn't always easy. Events come into our lives that deter us from our original direction. This is where we must screen out activities that will not advance our purpose and screen in things that will enhance our purpose.

Ask for Help

Collaborating with others is an important way to refresh our thinking and ask for ideas and thoughts that will enhance our mission or screen out activities that will take us away from focusing on our purpose. Listening to other ideas and questions is a healthy practice that brings clarity to what we want to do. Everyone knows this intellectually. Why don't we practice it? There are many reasons. Our egos inhibit us from asking for input. Maybe we think we are smarter than others and know exactly what to do. We frequently rationalize our way into deciding whether this is good for us or not. We just think we know best. And we may think we just don't have the time to collaborate and ask for input.

Rationalizing that you have made the right decision without exploring the right direction can waste a great deal of effort. Yes, you can make a faster decision if you think you know the right way to go, but the actions from the decisions you make may be outside of what will advance your purpose or mission. Moving ahead too fast can force you into something that may place you into a "swamp" that will take a great deal of energy to climb out of. As new situations appear in your work, slowing down, collaborating with others, and exploring the possibilities can save time as well as produce better results. Seeking clarity provides an opportunity to obtain an accurate perspective on reality and what is right for us or the situations we encounter. Do what is best.

Determine Your Resources

Consider the amount of time and other resources needed to complete the activity. Some activities will take longer than others, depending on the size of the project, desired results, and the quality or accuracy needed. It's important to collaborate with others sufficiently to determine the outcomes, resources needed, and who needs to be involved. You need to be equipped with the tools and time to accomplish the task. Remember, you are accountable and responsible for taking whatever actions are necessary to complete the task with appropriate quality in the required time. Make sense?

Enhancing my reputation requires me to produce high quality results for my clients. I can't afford to just get the work done. My standards for quality and my measurable outcomes force me to consider the most effective methods for taking my clients where they want to go.

Determine Your Desired Outcomes

The speed that you need to get the job done should be at a pace where you remain in control over how the activity is being accomplished. Feeling out of control frequently leads to confusion or overcommitment and not completing the work with the expected quality or accuracy. Working at a hectic pace takes its toll on *you* as well as the end results, especially if the results don't meet expectations.

Working at high speed adds to the confusion around you. The more confused you are, the more stressed you get and the more out of control you feel. This feeling is contagious. Others will also feel it.

Working at your peak pace does not mean you are working at your best. "Best" means:

- You are accomplishing a purposeful mission.

- You are thinking about better outcomes than originally designed and acting to generate them.

- You are providing the best products and services to your internal and external customers.

We have all felt out of control from time to time. Some of us may feel out of control *most* of the time. Being out of control is harmful; it leads to stress, human errors, and unproductive activities. This state can also lead to emotional breakdowns and mental health issues. Let's look at some common situations. We've all said this in the past: "There's no time to think!" "We must keep going as fast as we can." We place ourselves in situations where slowing down does not seem like an option. Others make demands on our time. We become busier and busier and then get out of control. We lose direction. We lose sight of why we are doing what we are doing. We start sacrificing our purpose, our personal lives, and the quality of our work. "No time to think" is a crisis situation. We must be aware of this or else we are heading for a disaster.

Controlling what is going on in your life is important for stability (and maybe for maintaining sanity). When your energy is focused, you stay in control. Of course, not everything is in your control. So be aware of what is beyond your control: for example, weather, economic conditions, senior management decisions, illness, aging, and, of course, taxes. You can talk about many of these areas, but, really, there is nothing you can do about them. You waste energy if you worry about such things too long. These elements of life beyond your control impact you of course, but at best, you can only prepare to handle the impact and make adjustments.

As previously discussed, busyness, multitasking, and overcommitting impact your level of control. This is energy draining. It's worse when you can't actually pin down why you are so busy. At times you may feel that you need to stay busy; something may be wrong if you're not really busy. You may even be afraid of not being busy. This feeling may be unhealthy, depending on the situation. If you feel this way, there is something wrong with the way you are doing your work or living your life. Take the initiative to analyze what is going wrong.

A purpose for your activities is extremely important. Without purpose you wander around, wasting time and energy. Being busy does not mean that you are productive or making a difference in the lives of the people you care about or your work. Moving ahead means that you know where you are going and how you will get there. You are in control.

Time to Pause

Name three of your biggest time-wasters.

What can you stop doing?

What short-term activities are you pursuing that have little effect on long-term goals?

What actions will you take?

2
Static Survival: Living Without Growth

Older versus Younger Generations

Early in our careers most of us struggled with how we would fit into the business world. We first tried to decide how we wanted our life to go. Then, we needed to try an occupation based on our education, talents, and background. But as we progressed in our careers, we tended to remain with companies for the long haul, whether they continued to be a good fit for us or not. Many of us may have changed areas and functions within the same company, but we tended to stick and plow through whatever came our way.

Older generations, in particular, seem to have trouble making choices for change based on where their talents could best be used. Most of us have allowed others to decide where we would serve the business or organization best. I'm sure business leaders have good reasons for placing people in certain roles, but *we* need to make sure that *we* are making the best career decisions for ourselves and our families, not just for others.

Conversely, generations X and Y (millennial) are more in control of their careers at younger ages. They seem to change roles and jobs more frequently than we did, placing themselves in a position of learning and growth as they design their lives. The corporate world has recognized their independent nature and is trying to change the culture in order to attract and retain the talented people in these generations. The companies that attract the younger talent have adjusted the dress code for a more casual work environment; they move people within the organization to help them learn at an accelerated rate; texting internally is an accepted way of communicating and exchanging information; and most of all, companies are showing that they care about the individual while helping them design his or her career path. New approaches to retaining talent are instituted monthly.

My career was an example of this until 2000, when I took control and decided to become a consultant and executive coach. I worked in seven companies before I decided to do what I really wanted to do in the next chapter of my life. I had previously thought that I wanted to have my own consulting firm. The year 2000 was the best possible time for me to start. I had the right experiences in my career to be able to help other businesses become better and more profitable than they were in the past. Executive coaching was another discipline that I was able to add to my services to my clients. The week I left my final corporate position, I started my coaching training at The Hudson Institute of Santa Barbara.

Inadvertent Change

I know that we are pleased when others ask us to help the organization in different roles. This is a way to learn and grow. Sometimes we surprise ourselves when we get promoted into jobs with more responsibilities and rewards. This is good if we are doing what is right for us and what we have planned regarding using our talents or following our passions. However, being promoted to a higher level or moving from an individual contributor to a manager role may not be good for us or the right role for our natural talents. For example: a great salesperson may turn out to be a poor sales manager. This is a common occurrence. A salesperson needs to consider his or her career plans first. Then senior managers must assess whether the natural talents of a great salesperson match the skills required of a successful manager.

Another type of situation besides being placed in the wrong role for our skills and talents may occur as we grow in our careers. Most of us have heard about the Peter Principle, meaning that people rise to the level of their incompetence. I don't believe in the Peter Principle. I believe that people rise to a level where they find themselves stuck, lacking energy and new knowledge, and become bored—but not to the level of their incompetence.

I had a client; I'll call him Bill. He was a director for many years. Bill's wakeup call came when he received some disappointing feedback from his boss and coworkers about his behavior and management abilities. He seemed surprised at the feedback. Senior management wasn't sure if he could manage the accelerated growth that they were about to execute. I was asked to coach him to lead and manage at a higher level. Bill described his situation this way. "There are firemen who are expected to put the fires out. The fire chief spends most of his time inspecting buildings and educating the owners to prevent fire and make sure the facility is safe. I was a fireman, and I needed to be a fire chief. I needed to be more proactive and less reactive." Bill was a valued employee who was very loyal and wanted to improve and contribute at a higher level.

He started making behavior changes after our first conversation. Bill's interactions became constructive. He showed more respect, became less reactive, learned to understand that everyone had different talents and they were all different from him. Bill started to let go. He delegated more; planned the projects, not the day-to-day activities; trained others to do the work he was doing; and was proactive about more long-term planning. Bill now says, "I am more productive, have less stress, am more confident, and can handle the pressures of the work much better. What I have learned spills over at home. My wife just told me last weekend that I am different, in a good way. My relationships with my direct reports, peers, other department heads, and my boss are much better. I used to work sixty hours a week. Now my hours are down to fifty or fifty-five hours, and I'm more productive, as well as taking on more strategic efforts."

Bill went beyond his "level of incompetence" and became a bigger contributor to the business. *He* decided the direction he wanted to go and developed a written plan for how to get there. Bill continues to help grow the business.

Static Survival

Danger lurks when we get comfortable, because we can get lazy about our own growth. I call being stuck in this situation *static survival.* We are surviving, not thriving. We get comfortable in our jobs or roles. Things seem to keep rolling along. We do our work, get a paycheck, get a "Meets Expectations" performance rating once a year, and receive the customary raise in salary. We are appreciated and feel safe in our job.

Be aware of where you are and what is going on around you. And then take action when you feel stuck. Why is that necessary? Why not just be comfortable? There are two reasons.

For one, if you continue in this static, comfortable manner, you can get fired for not growing with the work or expanding potential opportunities. Others will make the choice for you if you don't recognize it yourself. With the economic downturn, the business climate is becoming more aggressive and competitive than in the past as competition in the global economy increases. Consultants and colleagues have observed that during a financial crisis, companies lay off their mediocre performers. You can't afford to get stale in what you are doing professionally or your job may be in jeopardy.

Second, if you aren't growing, are you dying? Static survival mode in the business world can be a slow death unless you snap out of it and take action to learn what you need to learn to compete with others and to hone your skills to meet future business needs. When a business is in crisis, it's too late to learn *you* may be the next person to be laid off.

Moving Forward

Escaping static survival doesn't necessarily mean you have to leave your current company or start your own business. Start with small steps. Revisit the place where you are now in a new light. Write down what you do, why you do it, and how you are growing in what you do. After giving this some thought, if you don't like what you see, then it's time to move on. In Part II, I will show you in more detail how to reevaluate your current position and, if necessary, move on.

If your changed behavior isn't getting the results you want, and no one is listening or noticing, you probably need to make a more dramatic change. You may not be satisfied with the results of your current work. It's probably time to reassess your situation, make some choices, take action, or move on. This doesn't necessarily mean that you will leave your company. It means that you need to find another position that will fit your purpose and strengths. You want to engage those strengths for better use and impact the business in a different way. The business will benefit, and you will regain your enthusiasm for the work you do. It's a win-win. Thus, you advance your career.

Stuck in Our Stories

We've been discussing what it takes to move ahead by dealing with the truth and seeing reality clearly. Some of us have trouble seeing the truth because we've been in a static place in our lives for many years. The stories we tell ourselves may keep us stuck. We can't get off of the treadmill even though we are disenchanted with our life. We may be zombies every day. We could even keep telling ourselves that we are happy being stuck. We keep convincing ourselves and others that this is what life dealt us and we can't change things. It seems safe, but being stuck is like a sort of death. We just keep on walking in the rut. This is not a healthy way to live. People in this state are not looking for meaning in their life. They may have lost touch with what happiness and true joy mean.

Telling yourself "that's just the way it is" creates a circumstance void of hope. Resignation is like putting yourself in a box without any hope of getting out. Many times fear keeps people stuck. Take action if you see yourself in that situation. This is the time to search for more. Tell yourself that searching for possibilities to enrich your life is worthwhile. Life is not meant to be hopeless. It's in your control to decide that there is more for you to do. Sometimes you may think that you don't deserve more than you have. It could be that you are punishing yourself for something in the past. However you feel, you have the opportunity to take control and create a new story for your life and work and let go of the fears and barriers that hold you back.

Change Your Story, Change Your Life

Who creates static living? You may not recognize that it's you who keeps you where you are. Do you blame other people and unfortunate events for your current plight? Do you understand that if you change your story, you can move out of your rut and become unstuck? Tell yourself that you are going to get what you really want. Go for it, without guilt or ties to the past. This is where a purpose plan is so important. If you don't have a dream and a plan, you don't have any direction, and consequently you either place yourself on the treadmill or continue in a downward spiral.

Expand your world: dream. When you know what you really want, you create the stories that allow you to change your beliefs and think about the people in your life. You start changing your life when you rid yourself of the lies and assumptions you've been living with and replace them with new stories of renewal and growth and what you actually want. When you start making changes in your attitude and view of the future, others around you start reacting to your behavior in a favorable way. Others can also feel the "infection" for living differently. People notice that you are authentic and in control of the way you live. They tag along because they like your positive energy. They want to be around you. In this way you receive support for fulfilling your plan or purpose.

Limiting Your Potential

Frequently we place limitations on ourselves with the stories we weave. I've experienced it. I told myself when exercising that my maximum heart rate should be 136 bpm. I hired a personal trainer to strengthen my back, knees, and upper body and get me fit again. As he worked with me, he pushed me to do more and more. I finally talked about checking my heart rate. It was 155. I knew that I was progressing, but I didn't know I could safely go that high. Now, I get my heart rate over 150 once a week without any problem. I had told myself that I couldn't or shouldn't do more. After I cleared up the assumption, I progressed steadily. By the way, I have no pain in my knees, hips, or back anymore. I feel fit. I work out at least three times a week. I feel better about myself and my well-being. I am directing my energy in the right places. I corrected an assumption by taking some action. I learned from the actions and made positive adjustments that benefit me and others.

I know this is a simple example. Life is more complex. I am suggesting that the clarity you discover and the adjustments you make will simplify your life and work. You can rationalize that you must live in a fast-moving, complex environment. Is this another story you tell yourself? I just walked past the TV and heard Oprah say, "You need to really live in the truth. Life is too short."

Saying "I can't" is limiting. Wondering if you actually can is hopeful. Start telling yourself new stories that are believable. After rediscovering the truth about yourself and the way your life is playing out, tell yourself the new stories, the refreshing stories, the positive "can do" stories. These new stories will express your passion and help you pursue your real purpose. Good things enter your life when you express your passions. You now have clear outcomes in mind.

Change your stories and you will change your life. You have the power to change what you no longer want in your life. Many times it means forgiving yourself for the past. Forgive yourself for what you did not do as well. You may also need to forgive others in your life, but you won't be able to move forward unless you forgive yourself first. You only hurt yourself with your anger, disappointments, and misunderstandings. So, what's keeping you? Forgive and let go of the anger you embrace within you.

Letting Go

If you find you are living in a static state, you may first need to let go of fear and guilt in order to face change. Decide the value of what you want to take on, and then plan how you will move on. Honor the past, hold on to what is important, and let go of the less important activities and practices that no longer serve you.

What do you want to change in your life or work?

What values still hold true to your beliefs?

What do you need to let go of?

These may be difficult questions to answer. Beliefs that hold you back may need to change. Fears of making critical moves or decisions can hold you back for a lifetime if you don't face them. Slowing down to think about those fears, uncomfortable questions, and barriers can help you make some important choices. Are the barriers something that you can handle or manage to move out of the way? Spend time understanding what it will take to remove barriers.

Get Uncomfortable

Letting go of some of the things you thought were important is usually the most difficult part of self-renewal. Yet, by letting go you can develop the skills to move to the next level in your life or work, including a new profession. You may think you will lose something. You're right. At times growth means dropping some characteristics, plans, and "programs" that are lodged in your brain. Yes, eliminating some things within you that will not serve you or others in the future may mean a little "death." Let them go. Those unneeded characteristics must be replaced by something else that will shift your development into something new and exciting.

Many of us require some help getting beyond the aspects that need to be dropped. Ask for help! Sharing your thoughts with someone else is a way of processing. Choose someone you trust, a personal mentor or professional coach or therapist. He or she will ask questions you haven't thought about or question areas of your life and future that you may subconsciously not want to let go. Such uncomfortable questions are what you need. Get uncomfortable. Throughout my years of coaching and helping others, I have held to the concept that nothing really changes unless you get uncomfortable. Clients may become very uncomfortable and sometimes downright scared of what they need to see. Seeing things in a different light is a very helpful part of the process. It works. People move on when they get through the barriers of their own discomfort. People can not ignore reality if they want to make changes for their own growth and development.

Let Go of Guilt

Guilt is another emotion that holds people back from changing their lives. Rarely can you move ahead *with* guilt. Maybe you should say, "Enough! I've paid *enough* for my sins. I deserve to move on." You need to say and believe this in order to move on. If it helps, act out a ritual for letting go. Hold a funeral service for the guilty circumstance. Throw it in the garbage. Blow out the old candle: light a new candle. Guilt is something you allow to be trapped within. Yes, you allow it to keep you stuck. You can tell yourself that your mother, father, spouse, or another person is to blame. But it's you who allowed that to happen, and it's only you who can break the chain and say, "Enough."

Change Beliefs

Managing your life and work in a global economy may pressure you to make choices that lead you to letting go of things in your life and work that have no further value. This is tough to do, especially if you are a more traditional individual. Letting go of the past is something that is experienced every time you move into another chapter of your life and work. You will need to let go of some of the past. Don't forget about the past—you will always remember the significant events and what you've learned. Letting go of the past must include *respecting* the past for how it has served you. Of course, not everything in the past will serve you. "My company will take care of me" is a belief that most people let go of after 9/08, the financial disaster of September 2008. The reality is that most companies can't take care of you as they may have in the past. We must all take care of ourselves. Indeed, our country can't take care of us; even the countries of the European Union have experienced this, as entitlements have been lost. Our world has changed. We must make choices for ourselves now.

Some of the past no longer has value. Our beliefs must change. You need to change to thrive and grow. Doing what is right for you and your family will demand that you let go of "the way it used to be" and take different paths to meet tomorrow's needs in a global environment.

My Story

I have decided that certain things in my life are not worth struggling for. I thought I could be the top human resources executive in a large corporation. I let that go and started my own business. The goal of the head HR person seemed to attract too many problems for me and my family. I needed to refocus my energy on the things I valued most. The changes have resulted in not only a better relationship with my family, but a more meaningful course for me. I let it go. I decided that there were other challenges more important than a position and title. There were other ways of making the money. I needed to focus on the activities and things I needed in my life. I've never regretted my decision.

Life's Chapters versus Purpose

Planning and designing your future provides guidance and establishes clear goals, bringing meaning and purpose into your life.

There are times when we confuse our "chapter" goals and purposes with our lifetime goals. Chapter goals change as necessary when our environment changes. Lifetime goals are what we want in our lives for the rest of our lives; for example: enjoying our children and grandchildren; growing spiritually; continuing to contribute in some way until we die; staying healthy longer to enjoy ourselves without pain in our later years. All of these lifetime goals need attention at any age so that we can realize our dreams throughout our lives.

Our desires change with every chapter, and that's the time to change our direction or our chapter goals. Our needs change within every chapter as well. And, of course, our work life may need to change.

We should always consider our desires as well as our needs. We aren't honest with ourselves if we don't confront the reality of what's going on in this chapter of our career or life, including "what is the impact of a global economy and financial structure?" Ask yourself these "get ya goin'" questions:

- Am I in "static survival"?

- Am I stuck or afraid?

- Am I growing?

- What do I need to learn in order to continue to develop and grow?

- Do I still like what I am doing professionally?

- Am I feeling passionate about what I am doing?

Hopefully these questions will encourage you to slow down and take a look at where you are now. Then, do something to move ahead. Plan your life and purpose for your next chapter

Welcoming Adventure

If you are in static survival, accept the challenge and move ahead. Your life will be better for it. Be courageous, and challenge yourself with well-thought-out risks. Take control of your career. I know this process appears to take a lot of work and effort. Who said it was easy? It may even parallel the work it takes to get back in physical shape or lose ten pounds. Take the challenge and move ahead. It may be one of the healthiest experiences of your life. Of course, you can't follow your passions unless you know what they are. So explore them, create a new plan, and take action to make something happen.

Time to Pause

What stories are you holding that you need to clarify to discover if they are the truth?

Describe the new stories about how you will live your life and work.

Listen and then confront fears and beliefs that are barriers to you moving ahead.

Part II
Regaining Control

3
Models for Managing Change

Models are maps that describe a process that helps create a plan. The plan can be a personal purpose plan or a major project at work. A model is the structure that will direct a thoughtful examination process eventually leading to a design for your purpose plan.

Visual representations of models, pictures, and plans create an imprint in our mind. As we visualize what we want and how to get there, we integrate our emotions and feelings into the plan. The emotions are the motivation to maintain focus on our plan. Get excited about the journey. From our plan we develop initiatives that allow us to achieve our goals at work. Our personal lives take on the emotions and excitement for living our lives to the fullest, as well as living our lives as we've designed them. The pictures stimulate emotions, and emotions energize us to more forward.

There are many models to choose from. After looking at a variety of models, you can make a choice to use one that seems to work for your situation, or you can create a new model. This process may take some time and certainly some reflection, but seeking the right model is not as difficult as it may first seem. Let your values help make the choice. Values help you discover insight into what you may need before you integrate the insights into some form of structure: a model. Remember, you want to create a picture that reflects a structure for you to work in and help you achieve your purpose. I developed the Life Control Model™ for my clients, and you can create a model to help guide you.

Models for Personal Use
– A Life Chapter: The Cycle of Renewal

Let's review a few useful models. The model that I refer to most is The Cycle of Renewal. Fredric Hudson created The Cycle of Renewal and published it in his book, *The Handbook of Coaching.*[7] It is used extensively at The Hudson Institute of Santa Barbara. I use this model for myself, my clients, and my family members. Here's the model.

The Cycle of Renewal

A Life Chapter

Phase I:
"Go For It"

Phase II:
"The Doldrums"

Phase IV:
"Getting Ready"

Phase III:
"Cocooning"

© The Hudson Institute of Santa Barbara

A Life Transition

*Reprinted with permission from The Hudson Institute of Santa Barbara.

7   Hudson, Fredric, PhD *The Handbook of Coaching, A Comprehensive Resource Guide for Managers, Executives, Consultants and Human Resources Professionals*, Jossey-Bass Publishers, San Francisco, 1999.

A Life Chapter

The Cycle of Renewal asks, "Where are you in the model? What phase are you in now? What phase are you moving into?" Here's a review of the model.

"Going for it" is the phase used when we are passionate about what we are doing and everything seems to be working right for us. The "Doldrums" is when we are depressed or stuck in our life or work or both. We may not know what is happing to us, but we do know that something is wrong in our life.

"Cocooning" describes when we decide to get out of the Doldrums and change our life or work. This phase is meant to reflect who we really are: our strengths, desires, and needs. It's a time to seek God's guidance and search for what is right for us in the way our life or work needs to change.

"Getting ready" is the next step toward action, after we decide how our life will change and what we want to pursue. This is the time to prepare, unlearn, relearn, and seek help and resources to move ahead.

— William Bridges' Model for Change

William Bridges is well respected for his models for personal change. He describes "Endings" and "Beginnings" as important concepts to transitions in his book, *Managing Transitions, "Making the Most of Change"*.[8]

Bridges shows us that if we are going to move on, we need to let go of some things in our past or current situation. We need to seek new directions that will bring other things into our lives. We need to see the possibilities for us, our families, and our professional lives. Bridges describes that we are in all three phases at the same time, but we are in each phase in different degrees as we move through the change process. Moving on will mean leaving our comfort zone and getting uncomfortable about our future. "Nothing really changes unless you get uncomfortable"; my clients call this Bud's Law.

William Bridges' model is further explained by "The Seven Rules of

---

8   Bridges, William, *Managing Transitions, "Making the Most of Change,"* Addison-Wesley Publishing Company, 1991.

Transition Management," which pertain to organizational change. Look to see how the rules pertain to personal as well as organizational change.

1. You have to end before you begin.

2. Between the ending and the new beginning, there is a gap.

3. That gap can be creative.

4. Transition is developmental.

5. Transition is also a source of renewal.

6. People go through transitions at different speeds.

7. Most organizations are running a "transition deficit." (That means that under stress, people slide by and make a change without any real or personal transition.)

We've been discussing combining life and work models so you can understand that you can create a model for your chapter of your life or work, or both. You need to first look at the "whole you" and then look at models in context with your current life and work.

— *Cycle of Choices*

I developed the Cycle of Choices model to demonstrate the cycles of awareness of my clients' current situations and the choices facing them: to stay where they are or to move on to the next phase of change in their life and work. A "choice point" usually confronts most people. We all move through this cycle at the rate we choose. "Do I move on now? Do I stay where I am? How do I move on? "Where do I go?" The model is meant to help people make thoughtful choices. This model has helped me. It is a personal model that I use for guidance.

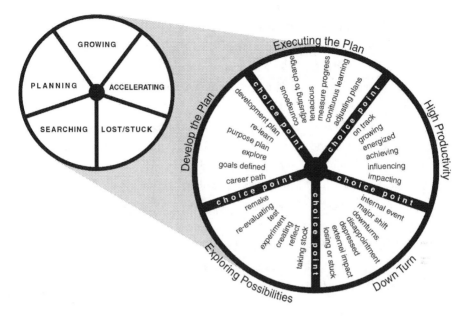

— *Phases for Current State*

High Productivity is where we'd like to stay all the time, but it isn't practical to think we remain there. Please don't confuse busyness for productivity. We've discussed this at length in previous chapters. High Productivity is the phase where we are energized, focused on priorities, and having a positive impact.

Downturns is the phase where things are negative and control is being lost. It is a depressed state because significant events have occurred that impact us in a bad way. These events may be out of your control, or you have made choices that have placed you in a bad situation.

— *Phases for Action*

Exploring Possibilities is where you actively make life and work adjustments. Your behaviors change. This is the time to ask for help, find mentors, or get coached about how you can effectively make the necessary adjustments. You need to explore areas of interest, test the waters, and get some advice.

This is where you may reinvent or transform yourself to meet the needs of the future. It's time to get creative with your life and/or work.

Developing the Plan is where you spend the time to write out a new plan. This is the time to make changes to your purpose plan and mission. You will spend time learning more about what you want to do and how to do it.

Executing the Plan is where you actively make life and work adjustments. Your behaviors will need to change. You will take more risks. You are moving toward your success. This is hard work and takes courage and persistence. Ask for help in your efforts toward executing your plan.

We make choices through every situation and phase. We need to be aware of where we are first. Then we can assess whether we need to move on or improve our current situation. I have devoted the entire next chapter to the Life Control Model™ that not only describes areas of control but the choices you have within your control.

Models for Business
— A Business Chapter: The Cycle of Renewal

In the model below, The Cycle of Renewal* is adapted to a business environment or a team environment. Phase 1, "Fully aligned," is optimistic, energizing, and passionate. Phase 2, "Out of Sync," is pessimistic, low-energy, resistant to change, and stuck. Phase 3, "Repurposing," is an organization's transformational phase for reinventing the business, accepting past loses, reevaluating your position, reflecting on "why are we in this business?" and whether it's time to change the culture, etc. "Exploring," Phase 4, is preparing for the next chapter in the organization, restructuring, process improvement, retooling, reeducation/training, high creativity, testing, experimenting, etc. It is not unusual that the Business Chapter model is similar to the Life Chapter model. Businesses operate in cycles. Teams operate in cycles. We personally operate in cycles of change. Both businesses and individuals need to renew themselves periodically.

The Cycle of Renewal

A Business Chapter

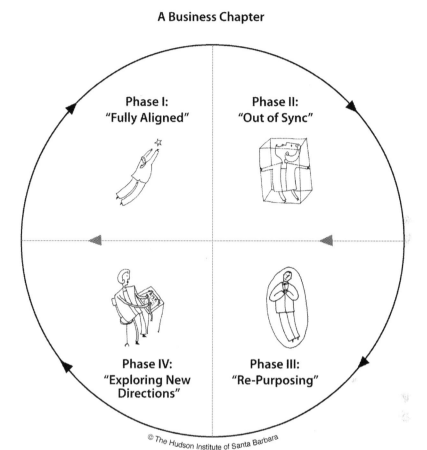

Phase I:
"Fully Aligned"

Phase II:
"Out of Sync"

Phase IV:
"Exploring New
Directions"

Phase III:
"Re-Purposing"

© The Hudson Institute of Santa Barbara

A Business Transition

*Reprinted with permission from The Hudson Institute of Santa Barbara

A Business Chapter

– Model for Creating Major Change

John Kotter's model for Creating Major Change in organizations has eight
critical steps, as described in his book, *Leading Change*[9]. Think about his

9   Kotter, John P. *Leading Change,* Harvard Business School Press, 1996.

suggestions for large-scale organizational change as it relates to you and your personal change efforts. Assess how the first five steps are related to your potential plan.

1. Establishing a sense of urgency

2. Creating the guiding coalition

3. Developing a vision and strategy

4. Communicating the change vision

5. Empowering broad-based action

6. Generating short-term wins

7. Consolidating gains and producing more change

8. Anchoring new approaches in the culture

The first five steps relate to personal change as well as large scale organizational changes. The last three pertain more to institutional activities.

— *Roth Model for Executing Change Initiatives*

I created the "Roth Model for Executing Change" by reviewing many models for change. I wanted a picture for moving the strategies for change and directing my clients to what they need to do to execute the strategies into actions.

Strategy	Execution
1. Clear vision, strategy, and communications	Create a picture, map the general course, and use frequent and candid communications.
2. Identify leaders for change	Assess, replace, develop, and reassign.
3. Get everyone involved and engaged	Institute a Steering Team, design teams to create new ways, and develop teamwork
4. Raise the bar and expectations	Performance objectives: expect results and accountability
5. Develop teams, leaders, and individuals	Live action coaching and facilitating, listen, help, teach, and reinforce
6. Energize and gain/keep momentum	Measure, seek short-term gains, share, have fun, and accelerate
7. Embed the new systems, practices, and organizational behaviors	Performance feedback; renew HR systems/practices and integrate the values into all activities
Strategy	**Execution**

The Roth Model is self-explanatory. I needed to show my clients how to get people moving in the same direction. My model is for smaller organizations' change initiatives, even department-size change efforts. You can also use a few of the activities in my model for executing your strategies.

– *Moving Through Change*

As you move through the changes you want to make, you will experience a variety of emotions. When you do, take time to try to understand what is happening within you. Confront the reality of the situation, and don't deny your feelings. You will probably experience setbacks, disappointments, and, of course, uncomfortable moments. You will also experience great joy, satisfaction, and many high points in your journey through your life's chapter.

The models and your plans will be your best maps and support. Ask for help when you need it. Seek out a trusted person to discuss what you are feeling.

– *Check It Out*

Checking your plan and models periodically is a good practice. Instead of leaving this "check-up" to chance, place it on your calendar. Make it happen. Time slips by quickly. The best thing about the check-up is that you will see your progress, and your purpose and mission will reinforce the fact that you have made the right choices for yourself. This reinforcement is important for giving you the energy and the courage to keep moving forward. External events will impact you. When they occur, you may have to make some adjustments to how you are executing your plans. Go ahead, make the adjustments. Your hand is on the tiller of your sailboat. This is how you stay in control of your life and work. Make clear choices for the actions you take. You will build confidence as you move ahead and continue to gain momentum.

Another Personal Model

Here is my example of a personal model. I encourage you to design the model that guides your intended direction. This guidance helps you remain in control.

What is my plan to change and get what I want?

What do I want?　　　　　　　What people and resources do I need?

What do I need?　　　　　　　What barriers do I see?

Who am I?　　　　　　　What is my executing plan?

Live My Plan

Time to Pause

Design a model for your life based on where you want to go and your purpose.

Establish milestones for measuring your progress to achieve your goals.

4

The Life Control Model™:

What You Can Control and What You Can't

I've have had a number of clients over the years who didn't think that there was much they could do to change their situation because too many things were out of their control. My job is to help them discover what they can control and act upon it to improve their capability. I encountered so many clients in this situation that I decided to graphically tell them what is *in* and *out* of their control. I created the Life Control Model for this purpose.

The model on the next page uses the metaphor of a sailboat. Read all of the words on the sailboat before you read the text that describes the model. Then, read the text and look back at the model to see where you see yourself to understand what is in your control.

The Life Control Model is designed to show that more is in our control than we think. This fast-changing world can frequently throw us out of control. We may feel that we can't make good choices for ourselves because of the situation in which we find ourselves. The Life Control Model allows us to see that we can regain control of our life. Take the helm in the areas in your life you can control, and be prepared for those you cannot.

The part that represents what is *out* of our control is represented by the wind hitting the sails. The rest of the sailboat represents everything *in* our control. That's because we control our lives similarly to the way we sail a boat.

Those of you who have sailed will relate to the control you have, even when you are in the doldrums; that is, when there is no wind or force pushing you forward.

Life Control Model™

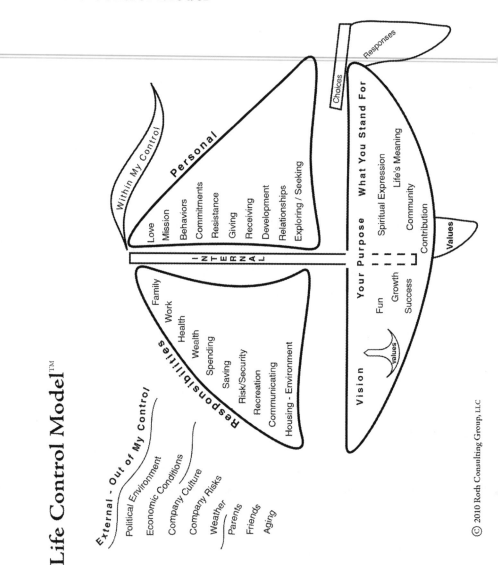

– *The five main elements of the model:*

- **The Wind:** External forces that are out of our control

- **The Jib and Main Sails:** Responsibilities and behaviors that are in our control

- **The Mast and Hull:** The mast is our internal strength, embedded in the boat hull, which represents who we are.

- **The Tiller and Rudder:** The choices we make are represented by the tiller, which leads to the rudder, or our responses.

- **The Keel:** Our values are the weight that we rely on to keep us upright and secure for making good choices.

Out of Our Control

– *The Wind in your sails*

The areas listed below are generally considered out of our control. These elements are represented by the wind and our sails engaging the wind. We must adjust to uncontrollable conditions or suffer the consequences.

Political environment	Weather
Economic conditions	Parents
Company culture	Friends
Company/competitive risks	Aging

In Our Control

– *The Mast: Your strength*

The mast holds the sails against the wind that can't be controlled. The mast is your internal strength mounted in the hull. The hull is the foundation of your character. The mast is required to support your responsibilities and personal behaviors every day. You succeed by using the sails to lean into the wind; together, they take you to your desired destination.

— The **Hull**: Who you are, your vision, your purpose, and what you stand for

Values	Spiritual expression
Fun	Life's meaning
Growth	Community
Success	Contribution

These areas of focus in the hull are the essence of who you *really are*. They describe who you are as a person. They are your authenticities, why you exist and "show up." This is the stable platform from which you initiate actions and how you respond to the challenges you face or opportunities you make for yourself. Slow down to consider what's in your control and what's in the hull of your sailboat.

Control of your life is based on your character, which is represented by the hull of the boat. You have gifts and strengths that you can use to accelerate achieving your goals and dreams. You need to be aware of these strengths, activate them, and move ahead.

You can't be great at everything. God didn't make humans that way. Be honest with yourself and decide what you can't be or do well. Those desires and characteristics may not be who you really are. How do you handle this? First, admit that you don't have the aptitude or interest in developing something in you that will take enormous energy. If you acquire the skills you need, you may not like how you are using these skills. Get some help to decide whether you have legitimate talents in the areas you think you want to pursue. Then make the choice to move ahead, with confidence.

You may want to transform your life into something completely different from what you've imagined in the past. This may be an opportunity to develop a hidden talent. The next step is discovering whether you are talented enough or truly interested in what you think you want to do. Slow down and take some time to explore this. You may want to change your mind or make other choices that are in alignment with your natural talents and interest. Acknowledge your limitations. Be honest with yourself. You can waste a great deal of energy pursuing something you are not.

We can make adjustments in how we achieve our purpose or make the life we want. I spend more time growing the strengths of my clients rather than focusing only on development needs. I can only grow weakness into a mediocre ability. However, I can help my clients take their strengths to the next level. They have the passion, talent, and positive energy to make leaps in growing what comes naturally to them.

Don't try to fit a square peg into a round hole. Your intended purpose will take you in the right directions, and you will make the right choices if you have been honest while developing your plans for the future.

— *The* **Keel***: Stabilizing factors in your life*

Your values are the weight that keeps your sailboat upright. The choices you make are based on your values. You should be able to depend on your values. They have been in place since you were in your youth. They may change over the years as you learn and experience different situations, but most of your values usually stick for a lifetime. You have learned to depend on them. Always depend on your values when making important choices.

You must also be aware that some of your values may not be good for you if they were established in a poor environment. Other factors may have generated values that are not good for the place you want to be or the environment in which you find yourself now. Spend some time reevaluating your values; drop the ones that won't work for you now, and replace some values that you feel are important to embrace. Your values help keep you upright—they are your keel. Values are your strength and provide the foundation for making decisions and choices that will impact you and your family. When bad, unexpected events occur, your values probably won't change because they express the stability within you.

Let your values guide how you will respond or behave. Be aware of the power your behavior has to influence events. Yes, I mean you have power! I believe that values drive behavior. Self-interested behavior may harm others. You may be making choices that help you but inadvertently harm others.

For example, one of Sally's values is to be successful in whatever she may do. She works hard and travels a lot as the VP of marketing at a $45 million company. She and her husband have two children, now thirteen and sixteen years old. Her husband has a full-time job as an information technology systems engineer. Both children are involved in athletics and other school activities. Sally's work responsibilities force her to miss about 75 percent of the school events. Her husband makes most of the events, but taking off work early to attend the children's activities is impacting his work with his development team.

In this case, it seems that everyone is negatively impacted: Sally's husband, the children, and Sally as well, because she is driven to success.

Your ego may be taking you beyond your values. Lack of caring for the well-being of others may twist your choices outside of the boundaries of how you want to "show up." You must be conscious of who you are, remain grounded in your values, and manage your values with balance and caring.

The keel, and the values it represents, is also important to get to your intended destination, or making the right choices. My friend, Larry Calihan said "Without a keel (values) a sailboat will move only where the "wind" drives it. Even if a person makes choices (tiller and rudder), they can only shift the angle at which the boat will run from the wind." We can be "out of control" if we don't consider our values when making life or work decisions.

Preparing to Launch

If we are planning to sail our boat, we need to be knowledgeable about every aspect of the vessel: the condition of the sails and rigging, auxiliary motor, safety gear, radio check, etc. Well, why shouldn't we be as well prepared for the journey we want to take with our life and work? We need to be prepared for making good choices that are in our control. If the weather is bad and the seas are rough, we will probably delay our sailing journey—a good choice.

You have designed the way you want to move forward for this time of life. Your values may be established for the rest of your life. Live your life with intention. Design your life and live it. This is called "authentically living your life." You're real. Make thoughtful choices in a straightforward manner. This way of living and behaving builds confidence and courage.

Lean into the Wind—Propel Yourself Forward

Leading a satisfying life means that you have become the best you can be. When you live life with this in mind, you influence others in a positive way just because of who you are and how you show up. Aspire to consistently show up the way you've intended. Don't wait years to become that person. Be that wonderful person right now! Live who you want to be now. If you want to change your life, be aware of your potential and change your choices. They are in your control; your hand is on the tiller of the boat.

You—Navigator, Sailor, and Captain

Be sure you are equipped with the necessary tools, knowledge, and mental fortitude before you undock and set sail. Your readiness for what you will do or where you will go is another important consideration. If you understand your purpose and mission, your talent, interests, and skill level, the choice may be clear; either "Yes, I'm ready," or "No, I'm not ready." This may not be the right time to move on this decision. You may need more preparation. Preparing for something you want to do can be an energetic and exciting time because you are exploring your passion and interests, taking actions that give you positive energy to grow.

During this preparation phase, while exploring what you want to do, you may experience confusion. This is normal. You need to test out what is true and what is not and identify what might be your fabrication of reality. You can rationalize the outcomes because you are anxious to get started on your new journey. Instead, be objective. Seek the facts that help you discern reality. Take a broad view of the situation, and develop some scenarios about what can happen in the future based on the truth, the facts, and your values. Take a tough view of the opportunities and possibilities. Don't place a halo around your future. That's rationalizing. Ask uncomfortable questions. Find honest answers. Then make the right choices based on your readiness to move ahead.

Being true to yourself means following principles that you already know are true for you. It takes courage to stand firmly on your principles. Courage comes into play when taking action. It takes courage to fulfill your plans. It takes courage to maintain meaning in your life. Step up and control the way you live life and perform your work. This will give you the confidence to make the right choices.

Tacking Through Life

Once in awhile, we are fortunate to have the wind at our backs, propelling us in the direction we want to go, but life, like the wind, often shifts unexpectedly. When it does, our role is that of the prepared sailor, tacking in the desired direction: that is, though the boat may be blown indirectly, from side to side, we must manage to keep it heading directly toward our destination.

Identifying those things that we can control and then being adequately prepared to handle them is the way to be ready for those changes that are outside of our control. For example, I live in tornado country. I can't wait for a tornado warning before I stock up on flashlights, batteries, water, the first aid kit, and toilet paper. I have to know what we need ahead of time—finding a shelter where I can take my family if a tornado is possible, for example—and then be prepared for action, if necessary. I need to have everything I need in a large bucket so I can grab it or stow it in the area of the basement where we will take cover. I need to control what we need to survive.

Another example is when my insurance agent suggested that we increase the amount of homeowners insurance because both the value of our house and building costs rose. We were in our home for five years. My wife hesitated to pay the higher premium, but it made sense to me, so we increased it to the amount our agent suggested. Six months later our house was struck by lightning, which started a fire in the attic. We didn't lose anything precious because most of the damage was from water. Regardless, we had to move out for seven and a half months while the house was being rebuilt. We were prepared for the financial hit. Thank God we had increased our insurance coverage. We were totally covered. We moved back into our home and lived there for another three years. The emotional hit was more concerning. We handled the trauma. We kept moving forward after the disaster set us back.

Navigating Your Way
— *The Tiller and Rudder*

There are situations and events that occur throughout the days, months, and years that test what you are made of and the person you really want to be. Slow down to refocus on what's really important to you, others, and your work.

At times, you need to let go of the choices you would like to make if those choices aren't in harmony with your purpose or mission. You will see more positive energy emerge if you make good choices and maybe forego certain short-term gratification for the sake of long-term goals for yourself, family, and work.

Changes in our lives may come frequently, especially in the changing business, economic, and political environments. Many of my business clients live in a frequently changing environment, especially when economic crises occur. In order to accept the changes we face, we need to first decide how we will react to the changes that challenge our status quo. How we respond to these changes is our choice. These choices are based on our values, as well as the plans we have for ourselves. Use these to make the best possible choices: first our responses and then our actions.

Slowing down will improve the quality of choices. Questions you ask yourself are critical to thinking, analyzing, and choosing. Confront any conflicts head on. Ask questions. Collect more information. Seek out help or advice. Revisit your values, beliefs, and goals periodically to get back on track while navigating to your destination.

— *The **Tiller**: Choices*

Your hand is always on the tiller. Coordinating your use of the tiller with managing the sails will determine just how well you navigate through the daily situations and opportunities you face. You make choices about the actions you take and how you respond every hour of the day, throughout your life.

– The **Rudder**: *Responses*

Control your behavior and responses when unexpected weather comes. Your responses are the results or consequences of the choices you make. We all have choices to make about actions within our control. Make it happen! Coordinate the plan. Make choices and take actions as you would manage the sails, wind, and tiller.

– The **Jib** and **Mainsail**

All of the elements below are in our control. We must manage them well to adjust to the uncontrollable elements that we encounter. We manage the sails to take advantage or adjust to weather conditions. The *jib* represents our responsibilities. The *mainsail* reflects elements of how we respond to growth opportunities and behaviors that influence our abilities to manage our responsibilities and personal life.

Responsibilities—the Jib

Family	Saving
Work	Risk/Security
Health	Recreation
Wealth	Communicating
Spending	Housing—Environment

The jib isn't moved as frequently as the mainsail. The jib represents more stable elements of our life, the fundamental foundation of our responsibilities.

Personal—the Mainsail

Love	Commitments	Relationships
Mission	Resistance	Development
Behaviors	Giving	
Exploring/Seeking	Receiving	

The mainsail is maneuvered more frequently than the jib: we use it to tack back and forth to leverage the wind so we adjust the speed and move toward the destination. We make more frequent choices about our day-to-day behaviors. Controlling our own behavior is part of controlling what we can control. We can't control the behavior of others. We need to know what we can control, and that is our own behavior. We're able to influence but not control others by the way we react and behave. There is always a choice as to how we will behave or respond. Remember to slow down, process what is really going on, and make the choice about how to respond. We have the power to change the course of events just by making the right choices about how we should respond.

You have the tiller in your hand. It's your choice. Others will respond to your behavior, which will influence others without telling them how they should behave. You don't have control over others' behavior, but you can influence their behavior. You know what is right. You can make good choices that help you as well as those whom you touch and influence.

Navigation Check

Renew your plans periodically, especially when events out of your control occur. This is the time to make adjustments to portions of the plan, understanding that you will not sacrifice what you stand for. If you lose your job, your family may have to cut back on expenses, but everyone is still working together to focus on what is really important: safety, love, spiritual needs, a sense of belonging, etc. Your family counts on you to be in control of what you can control. They need to be confident that you will be the same person you were before the unexpected event. Your fundamental values are most important at this point. They are your anchor. Don't forget who you are and what you stand for. Internal emotional fortitude is going to help you move on, renew your plan, and take action to achieve the next phase of your life.

Time to Pause *(Drop anchor for awhile.)*

Review the Life Control Model sailboat. Assess how you are responding to what is out of your control. Then, identify what is in your control that you previously thought was out of your control.

What do you need to investigate first in order to make a course change in your life and work?

5

Slow Down to be More Productive

Slowing down occurs when you pay attention to what is going on around you. Slowing down actually helps you become *more* engaged. You ask more questions. You look into the events for insight. You get as excited as others are about what is happening in *their* lives. You share important thoughts, feelings, and experiences when you slow down. I also believe you won't leave as much undone or incomplete if you slow down to hold a good conversation and develop understanding.

Slow down enough to talk with others, and make choices that most people can buy into. Teams typically try to reach a consensus decision about solving problems or implementing activities that take them closer to desired outcomes. As many of you may know, consensus takes longer than making unilateral choices and decisions. At the same time, consensus-driven decisions usually produce better results. Slowing down to talk and even have discussions around conflicting views is healthy and can bring out the best thinking. These are opportunities that lead to a deeper level of understanding and produce better outcomes.

Do you know when you are out of control? Do you slow down enough to feel the anxiety created when you are out of control? How does your body feel when you're losing control? It is frequently stressed, causing you to be nonproductive. Stay in control by focusing on the highest priorities and the intended outcomes. Then move ahead with confidence. Slowing down helps you assess the situation.

When you slip out of control, ask yourself these questions:

Why am I doing this?
Where am I really heading?
What is my purpose or mission?

By now you know the other questions to ask yourself. Sometimes busyness creeps into your life. When you notice this, it's time to slow down and take a clear look at where you are headed and get back to purposeful activities.

Slowing down is helpful for getting back in control of your life and work. Take a deep breath; think and seek perspective on what is happening around you. Write down your thoughts as you are exploring how to get back in control. This will help you be clear and to get unstuck. To save you from continuing to waste energy, just write about what is happening to you. Write down what is really important to you. Figure out what has crept into your life and work and start discarding some of the activities that don't really matter.

Ask yourself, "For the sake of what?" Asking this question will allow you to center your thoughts and activities. Of course, you want all of your activities to be purposeful, even if they are strictly for entertainment and relaxation. You make better choices about how you use time if you frequently ask, "What's the purpose of doing this?" Think of time as currency. Where are you going to spend this currency of time? How do you get the most out of your investment of time? Time is a consumable resource. You need to make good choices as to how time is spent. Focusing and refocusing your activities provides a reliable platform for making the choices that move the business ahead. That is why it's important to ask, "For the sake of what?" The answer clears up many assumptions we may have.

When you are *not* living with assumptions, you start becoming more productive. Too many assumptions in your life disguise reality and cause you to avoid the truth and waste your time. Subconsciously, when your vision is clear and barriers are removed, you move to where you want to go. Dealing in reality identifies barriers as well as opportunities and possibilities. You stop wasting energy and start putting your positive and passionate energy to work for you. Start feeling the freedom that this clarity brings. Your life should become filled with satisfaction from the things you are doing now. Be confident that you can do the things you want to do, and move ahead with passion.

Productive and Meaningful Work

Purposeful activities, projects, and strategies produce meaningful work. Purpose provides energy as well as focus. When working toward the purpose of an activity you really want to accomplish, a great deal of energy is generated to complete it. Meaningful work instills a passion for what you do. Passion produces high quality work, as well as accomplishing the objective or goal. This work is meaningful to your values, pride, quality, expectations, and high standards.

Not focusing on *what's important* in the life you lead can take you off track from your intended journey. Think about when you're driving a car in the fast lane on the freeway. You drive as fast as you can because you don't want to waste time. But you may miss the beauty along the sides of the road.

- What is really important for you to be doing?
- Are you focused on meaningful activities?
- What could you be missing that you may regret in the future?
- Are you wandering from your intended mission or priorities?
- How do you compare driving a car in the fast lane to driving your life?

Living in the fast lane, like driving in the fast lane, is something you can control. No one is telling you that you must live this way; *you* make these choices. Moving or working at a high speed may warp your sense of reality. Ask yourself if you are missing the meaning behind what you are living and working toward. This is why I suggest that you slow down and review your personal and professional lives.

Focus on purpose and mission to be productive. This intentional, meaningful way of living will keep your attention on the kind of life you want to live. It also fosters love and attention for and with the people who bring meaning into your life. Make better decisions for yourself, your family, and your business activities by knowing and understanding why you are living and working the way you are. Making a difference is something you may desire. Focusing on your purpose leads to good choices. It also screens out wasted efforts, busyness, or initiatives that take you in the wrong direction, wasting energy and resources.

Business or Busyness?

You make a greater impact on productive work by focusing on the activities and priorities. Focusing is more productive in the long run than just staying busy with many little tasks. Numerous little tasks can trap you in the busyness of the work and keep you from being as productive with meaningful activities. This is a paradox. When you feel like you are on a treadmill, you are into busyness. You've probably noticed this. You frequently miss this and don't take actions to change it. Aren't you looking for results: meaningful outcomes that impact the business?

Slowing down to ask yourself some important questions will help you reach the productive levels you would like to achieve and sustain.

- Am I really being productive or am I just into busyness?
- Does multitasking make me more productive?
- How am I impacting the goals of the business?
- Is what I am doing aligned with the goals of my department or company?
- Am I going to make a difference today by the work I will do?
- Am I just doing what I'm told to do?
- Am I thinking about how to do my work better?

The answers will lead you to more investigation and later to actions to change your patterns of how you work.

As we've discussed, multitasking is a common activity that can fool you into thinking you are productive. Maybe being very busy and getting many tasks completed feels productive, but to what end? Ask yourself how you are moving the project forward. I believe multitasking is unnatural and harmful for human beings. It creates emotional stress that eventually breaks down your effectiveness. It's an illusion to think multitasking is productive. An example of how unproductive multitasking can be is when you are answering and sending e-mails most of the day. Is your work frequently interrupted by incoming e-mails? When the incoming e-mail tone sounds, do you stop and read the e-mail, and then go back to the task you have already started? These distractions can go on all day if you let them. Important and productive work may be diluted because your thoughts and time were filled with interruptions. This is in your control. How can you control this simple activity and be more productive? Maybe e-mails can read in the early morning, after lunch, and at the end of the day. It's just a suggestion. Find your own solutions, but control your time.

Busyness and Productivity

Let's contrast busyness and productivity. We can be busy working on the highest impact activities. We can also be busy with many unrelated tasks. Have you ever stopped to take a breath and ask yourself why you are doing something, whether it is making a difference, or if it seems really ridiculous to do? Sure you have. We all have. Many times we do something without thinking much about it. Busyness suffocates creativity and unplugs the connection between the outcome of the project, mission, or work. If you don't slow down to think clearly and collaborate with others, you may start heading in the wrong direction and miss the best ways to implement your actions.

Texting and social media are other sources of ongoing distraction. I understand that texting is replacing some internal e-mail communications, but texting has the same interruption potential as e-mail. The number of e-mails and calls handled doesn't mean you are productive. Please think about how to manage yourself differently to be more productive.

Busyness may be encouraged when you hear; "You need to do more with less." Bosses, CEOs, and CFOs want to reduce costs and become more efficient. You're expected to improve your processes and work habits. You receive performance ratings based on productivity. So your productivity eventually shows up on paper. Maybe the measures your bosses use aren't what you would like. I suggest you measure productivity for yourself. This doesn't mean to just stay busy. I want you to think about why your task needs to be done, not to just do it. You need to do or say something when you are being led or pressured into performing unproductive work. This work you allow into your day may not be making a difference in moving toward your goals or the mission at work. What can you do?

If you are a customer service agent, do you measure productivity by the number of customers helped or sold in a day? Stop and ask yourself, "Was the customer really satisfied with the help?" or "Will the customer buy from the company again because of the way I helped them?" Place yourself in the customer's shoes to answer these questions. You've experienced surveys asking you, the customer, if you were satisfied with the way the agent helped you. These are good measures that make customer service agents better and let you know how you are impacting the business. Measures, surveys, and questions check the reality of how the customer is helped. Past customers only buy from you again if they were satisfied with the service, as well as the product.

There are things you can do to control your work environment to meet the objectives of the mission. Spend some time thinking about and discussing this chapter with others. This is the first step in being more productive. You have slowed down to learn how you can become more productive in your work. Become aware of your situation. You are starting to ask yourself questions you may not have asked before. You are starting to search for answers and the possibilities that make your work, and life, more satisfying and successful. Let's first look at some important concepts as we move forward.

Questions Seek Reality

"For the sake of what?" may be a tough question at times. Yes! Ask tough questions; it's healthy. Seek the truth. The tough questions will keep you focused on your purpose. Confronting reality is the way to remove the barriers you encounter. We've discussed how helpful it is to confront the things that are standing in your way. Being silent can also be harmful to you, your family, or your business. Say what needs to be said. You are actually obligated to confront things at work that are unclear or activities that have no real purpose. Ask the questions that confront reality. At work it's prudent to be politically sensitive, but this only means that you need to take a politically appropriate approach to asking uncomfortable questions.

Get the Best Thinking

Collaboration is slower than merely deciding what should be done on your own. But the authoritative approach rarely produces the best thinking or the best results, unless the decision maker is exceptionally expert or knowledgeable. Listen to others, and learn together as you process facts, information, and ideas. You learn when you listen. You help others understand when you answer questions. Collaborating also allows others to be part of the decision-making process. Everyone wants to be heard. As the work or project progresses, people will take some initiative to do their best work when they feel they have ownership. When they understand the purpose of the work, they can find the connection to become part of that purpose. They can call the results their own as they fulfill the objectives. Better decisions are made when you have some ownership; it's personal. High quality work will occur with little wasted effort if you understand the part you play and feel accountable for the results.

Saying No

Questioning the reasons for the effort provides information that helps you become fully engaged, thinking about how you can best get the task or project completed. You may discover through questions that the rationale doesn't fit the objective. The task may be a waste of time and energy. Well, now what do you do? Say no? First try to discuss the situation openly with whomever is involved, including the manager who requested the activity.

How do you say "no"? There are a variety of ways. I suggest you help the other person understand. I can give you a few suggestions, but you can think of other ways of saying, "Let's slow down and look at some other possible alternatives to the task at hand." Ask some more questions to get to the core reason for the request. Don't simply refuse to do a task that doesn't make sense. More information is needed to focus the situation. You want to help the person requesting the task to process why this needs to be done and/or seek alternatives.

Discovering the core reason for some requests is actually your obligation if you are accountable for doing the best you can do for your employer or customer. Eventually, you help the requestor to see things in another light. You then may all agree that the effort doesn't really add much value. This conversation is helpful and leads to producing a better outcome or stops wasting resources. Questions add value. Ask how the task is aligned with the mission or the purpose of the project. Ask how the investment will impact the outcomes.

Resistance from others to questions about the request is common. It takes courage to push back and ask questions about the purpose of the task.

When I've asked my clients to take this step with their boss, they report that the results were positive 90 percent of the time. Either they understand the reasons for the actions much better or the boss saw the light and changed his or her mind, perhaps suggesting another action that made more sense. "Wow! It really worked!" is the frequent comment.

It takes courage to see reality and ask tough questions. People respect the fact that you want to focus on the priorities. Ask questions around those priorities. You will eventually progress to the reality of the situation.

Managing Your Leadership Methods

Most bosses don't want to over-control their associates, but controlling-type managers usually want to gain confidence in others before they let them go on their own. They give orders and then tell you how to do the work. Other bosses are perfectionists and sometimes want to have their fingerprints on the outcomes. Some managers want to continue doing the work they like to do because they are good at it. Questioning these types of leaders is more helpful to them and the business than most of us may think. If you are a "controlling-type" manager, you can learn to let go and start working on more important things and still have the control needed to lead people to their best work. Try to stay more strategic. Focus on the priorities that are linked to the strategy and purpose. Help people by avoiding nonessential tasks that interrupt the focus or flow of the work. You as a leader can also let go by providing the mentoring and resources to your people to get the job done. "Teach them to fish." First lead; then mentor, coach, and provide support.

My client, Steve, is an area director for six retail outlets. He was in the habit of giving his managers the answers to their questions immediately and providing a solution to the problem. I asked Steve to stop telling and start coaching the managers by asking questions. The next week, while visiting a location, two managers discussed a personnel issue about behavior issues with one of the workers. The managers wanted Steve to provide the solution as he had in the past. This time Steve asked them what *they* thought they should do. He asked for some alternatives without sharing his thoughts. The two managers eventually came up with a corrective action that was even better than what Steve was thinking of. The two managers then owned the problem *and* the solution.

The result was that the worker with the behavior issues became the top performer in that outlet within a short period of time. The two managers felt more confident from Steve's empowerment.

You may be a leader who is apprehensive because you don't know how to move forward because you think you must have all of the answers. Just have the conversation. We've discussed the importance of collaborating. Asking for help is collaborating. Don't get hung up on your need to make all decisions or be the expert or make the best choices. Ask others for help. Don't waste time and resources delaying a project or guessing at how the work will get done. Ask for help from your people, other colleagues, and experts. Think of this as a way of learning, of helping others contribute and learn along with you. Get your ego out of the way; it could be your biggest barrier.

Short Term or Long Term?

Your real purpose at home and at work is to focus on the long-term results, not just the short-term projects and tasks that can fill up your day. Ask yourself:

What is the real purpose of all that I am doing?

What will my boss say when I am letting so many other things suck up my energy that I miss the objectives?

It's not your boss or even your wife that you are accountable to; it's *you*. *You* need to be honest enough to focus on the long-term and have the courage to manage your life in a better way. Say no when you're about to overcommit. Stay with the plan by focusing on the highest priorities. Of course, you need to be aware of the politics at work. Politics can lead you and others astray. It takes courage to avoid political pressure in any organization. You can't ignore the politics, but you can't let politics overshadow the reality of your long-term mission and short-term strategies.

Annual strategies guide the development of tactical activities for the year, which eventually get you to the actual long-term objectives. You are really looking for long-term results or solutions. Businesses usually move in cycles. Business cycles, or chapters, are similar to personal chapters in life. The long-term goals of a business chapter may be three to five years out. Annual strategies in your life help to focus on what you want to accomplish in the short-term. You also make adjustments to your personal plan depending on the pressures occurring at home or significant changes in your work. Then the cycle repeats itself.

Picture the future within the chapter you designed. This drives your intentions throughout the months and the year so you can accomplish what you want in your life in that chapter. The written plan, the strategy, and the pictures you design provide the focus for you to make the daily choices that take you to where you really want to go during the year.

Asking Yourself Questions

Truth is found through the questions you ask yourself. You can only get to the core of issues and truths if you ask questions that may be difficult and, at times, uncomfortable. Uncomfortable feelings or experiences stimulate change and appropriately pressure you to think and take action. Get to the core of what you are all about and what you want. The honesty you bring forth will lead you to the right answers or solutions for issues with which you may be struggling.

Where are you going?

What is your purpose or mission?

How can you focus priorities when so much is expected of you?

Why are you overloaded?

Questions such as these need to be asked, no matter what life you are leading or what stage of life you are in. Stay-at-home spouses, volunteers, retired workers of any generation; those in transition; independently wealthy people; all should be asking themselves these questions, searching for answers and planning the next phase of their life.

"Why?" This is a great question. Many times we are intimidated by others and inhibited from asking this question. Self-criticism leads us to thinking that what we want to ask is dumb. Take a risk; ask the question. Asking why is an appropriate approach that starts people thinking. If we ask why, we help ourselves and our colleagues. We gain understanding of the purpose and will probably produce better results. Periodically revisiting the purpose of the project or mission helps to regain clarity and focus. We don't want to get trapped by something that doesn't make sense and will eventually become unproductive work.

These thoughts are also meant to be applied to our family. Asking yourself and others why you are living your life in this manner is key to focusing on purposeful activities and holding very important conversations. Conversations with your spouse can lead to refreshing your relationship. You might discuss how to better raise the children or take parenting to the next level. Try it.

Confronting the reality about why you are living and working the way you do is at times uncomfortable. You must take risks to make the important changes in your life and work. Get uncomfortable! Bud's law is "Nothing really changes unless you get uncomfortable." So, get uncomfortable and take control of your life. Take action on the important choices you make for yourself. Get moving in the direction you want to go. You will find that some people will start following you, but that's not as important as you standing up for what you know is right. That's right. I'm suggesting that you need to stand up for what you believe. You will make a difference in this world and in the lives of those you touch

Confront Traditional Paradigms

To gain a clear perspective of what is really important to you, you will need to learn to do the following:

- Confront traditional paradigms
- Confront programmed thinking (hard-wiring)
- Engage in exercises for taking action
- Create the quiet, personal environment needed to slow down to think about what is important in both your home and work lives

Let's take a look at some fundamental elements in your life. As I've previously discussed, you can't plan out your entire life, as did your parents or those who lived in the Traditional Generation. The world is changing too rapidly. I thought at one time that my children should stay with a company long enough to learn, work, and achieve something so they could have a great-looking resume describing a stable career path. I've changed my thinking. All of my three children have chosen a variety of career opportunities and made changes in companies much faster than I did. They are doing fine and pursuing the lives that they want for themselves and their families. It's not perfect and not without some pain, but they are living out their plans while continuing to explore opportunities. They continue to make changes that are aligned with their purpose and their plan.

Ask Questions of Others (Collaborate)
– *Confronting Barriers*

We create barriers to achieving what we really want in many different ways. We've been discussing how to confront yourself and discover the truth about yourself. We've also discussed asking others to help clear your thoughts and get back on track. You may now need to also confront the people who may be barriers to your progress. Sometimes you can dance around the truth, make up stories about another person, and avoid confronting the person with the issue. Don't delay actions or avoid the situation. Clear up assumptions about those with whom you have a conflict. You could be wrong. You could be assuming you know the truth. It's time to seek the truth by raising the issue with the other person. Have courage; this will be uncomfortable. The following approach may take some of the fear out of confronting a thorny issue.

Tell the person what you have observed, or share the information you have. Then describe how that impacts you and possibly others. Then just listen to the other person. Dig for the truth. After you both know the truth, change the focus to your common purpose—what you both want. You and the other person will probably both make some adjustment in your behaviors, expectations, or actions. This process is effective for clearing up assumptions, dealing with reality, taking appropriate corrective actions, and forming new agreements.

Yes, you will need to be uncomfortable to follow this process initially, but you will be rewarded for your courage. Listen to the other person's view. He or she has probably also made some assumptions. Be patient as well as persistent to seek information and progress to a better understanding. Kerry Patterson, Joseph Grenny, Ron McMillan and Al Switzler, the authors of *Crucial Conversations*,[10] discuss the value of humility during barrier-removing conversations. "Confidence does not equate to arrogance or pigheadedness. Skilled people are confident that they have something to say, but also realize that others have valuable input. They are humble enough to realize that they don't have a monopoly on the truth. Their opinions provide a starting point but not the final work. They may currently believe something but realize that with new information they may change their minds. This means they're willing to both express their opinions and encourage others to do the same."

— *Find Mutual Purpose*

Collaborating with others is a great way to address assumptions and clear the way for the right decisions, actions, or activities. Not all conversations need to be confrontational. You need to know others in order to understand them. When you understand who they are, what their needs are and how they represent themselves, you will know what they want. You can deal with

10 Patterson, Kerry McMillan, Ron Grenny, Joseph, and Switzler, Al, *Crucial Conversations, Tools for Talking When Stakes are High*, McGraw-Hill, 2002.

others more effectively when you know their style and their motives. Your purpose is to find common ground, common understanding, and mutual purpose. Frequently, other people need to get to know us better. In this case, take the initiative to share who you are, what you represent, and what you need or want. This may only involve a couple of conversations to share each other's thoughts. Slowing down to have these essential conversations is an investment that usually offers great rewards. Building relationships allows you to gain cooperation from a variety of types of people.

I have been amazed throughout my careers, both corporate and consulting, that leaders don't engage in dialogue nearly as much as they should. I have guided many executives to talk with others to clear up issues, assumptions, and fears. It seems as though dialogue is a lost art. People appear to be too busy to hold in-depth discussions based on collective thinking and the intelligence of the group.

Daniel Yankelovich, author of *The Magic of Dialogue,*[11] writes, "Significantly, success at dialogue is much more self-evident than failure. When dialogue is done well, the results can be extraordinary: Long-standing stereotypes dissolved, mistrust overcome, mutual understanding achieved, visions shaped and grounded in shared purpose, people previously at odds with one another aligned on objectives and strategies, new common ground discovered, new perspective and insights gained, new levels of creativity stimulated, and bonds of communication strengthened."

Yankelovich's "Strategies for Successful Dialogue" are worthy of mention. His strategies are explained in detail in his book. Three core principles he suggests for dialogue are "equality, empathy, and openness." These principles apply as we strive to create a safe climate, clear up assumptions, use facts when identifying issues, explore trust issues that could result in misunderstandings, and identify common interests and positions. When engaging in good dialogue, you want to end up with a new agreement about how you and your colleague or colleagues will move ahead. Once made, you must keep your agreement; it's a commitment. At this point, all involved have their integrity on the line. Keep your commitments after you agree on mutually beneficial actions.

---

11 Yankelovich, Daniel, *The Magic of Dialogue, Transforming Conflict into Cooperation,* First Touchstone, 2001.

Time to Pause

Try these exercises to measure productivity.

Take time to think about how you can be more productive by controlling your work environment. Ask yourself about the time you waste. It's within your control to manage this important issue. Take the opportunity to make some changes in the way you work.

Answer the question "What am I doing that wastes time?"

Spend the next two weeks recording the work you do hour by hour. Develop a spreadsheet that you can complete as the day progresses. Review your morning's work before lunch. Repeat the review at the end of the day. At the end of two weeks, summarize what you have worked on as a percentage of that day. Identify the wasted or unproductive time. Later, decide if the work you completed made any difference to the goals of your department or business. This exercise is a laborious process, but stick with it. Two weeks will provide the information you need to make significant changes; don't perform this exercise longer than that. Then, make adjustments. Stop doing some things. Discuss areas of waste and value with your boss and coworkers. Choose to do the work that adds value and supports the current mission.

Contrast your busiest days with the days you feel you accomplish the most. What was the difference in the ways you were working?

Contrast how you felt about what you accomplished last Saturday when doing your errands with what you accomplished last Friday under the pressures at work.

What work habits can you control and change to make your day more productive, less stressful?

6

Slow Down for Your Well-Being

As you begin to look forward, first reflect on you alone; next integrate your family and then your work life. It's important to take care of yourself *first*. We frequently think that we are responsible for taking care of others and work before ourselves. "First things first" to me means to take a look at yourself *first*. It is easy to skip your own needs and make sacrifices for the sake of others. This sacrifice will not only prevent you from living the life you want, but you will be unable to effectively take care of others as you would like. Let's find a better way of taking care of you, your family, *and* your business, an approach that works for everyone to the best of your ability.

Take Care of Yourself First

Think about what is best for you before thinking about family and work. Of course you won't just forget about your family. Just take care of being healthy and on the right path, and then everything else will fall into place more easily. Be better prepared to take your family, relationships, and career to a higher level. Natural behaviors will emerge in most situations when you are confident about doing the right things for yourself and your family.

Taking care of yourself helps equip you emotionally to better take care of others. Consider your love for your family. You fulfill the needs of others, giving them your time, attention, care, and love. Your support is more authentic when you care for others from the inside out. If you don't take a close look at yourself and make important changes in your life and work, you won't demonstrate the value you can share on the outside. You will give yourself freely when you are satisfied with the way you are living *your* life.

There are many things you can do to take care of yourself. Refocus on your purpose and mission and what really matters to you. Refresh yourself by understanding how important it is to *personally* work toward what you want and need in your life. This focus will help you make choices for yourself and others in order to stay on course. You can choose to screen out the tasks and activities that will not advance your purpose. It's not much different from focusing on the annual business strategy. If you stray too far from the strategy, you won't accomplish what you set out to achieve for the year.

Challenges You Face

— *Focus*

When you feel that you are straying off course or your thoughts or activities are scattered and you have trouble piecing the "puzzle" together, then your stress level is out of control. That's bad stress as opposed to healthy stress. Healthy stress might be summed up as: "I feel energized and passionate about what I do. That's why I work hard or get into work early. I am not sacrificing my personal relationships because of what I do and the way I do it." Good stress means executing plans to complete your mission. You know where you are going, you know how you are going to get there, and you know that you are making a difference in the end. You are passionate.

— *Productivity*

By evaluating your productivity on a regular basis you will be able to refrain from overcommitting. Focusing on purposeful activities that move you toward the best outcomes will prevent you from getting sucked into overcommitting. Overcommitment frequently leads to a stressful, "out of control" condition. Stay clear of that trap. Ask the tough questions again if you start feeling pressured to do more than you should be doing to produce high quality outcomes.

— *Reality*

Facing reality and truth by confronting meaningless activities may help you avoid worthless commitments and busyness. Confront confusion about where you want to go. Looking at what is really happening or could happen is important. The things that slow you down on your way to your destination are worth assessing. "What is happening?" is a simple question that can reveal wasteful activities. If you don't slow down to take a deeper look, you may pass up a great opportunity. You may analyze the situation and identify a solution to a temporary barrier or a missed opportunity.

— *Change*

Instinctively when you are facing change or new circumstances, you first think of the potential personal impacts. This is the perfect place to be. Taking care of you first is key to taking control of what you can control. Choices as to what will work for you and what won't work for you will confront you. Then make course adjustments, while staying on track for your primary direction and purpose. Periodic reviews of your direction may be necessary to stay focused on actions necessary to fulfill the mission. Revisit the questions you've asked yourself in the past when you've slowed down to do a navigation check.

A colleague of mine, Hayden M. Hayden, shared his insight with me. "The quality of our lives is directly proportionate to the quality of questions we ask ourselves and others." These may be uncomfortable questions to ask, but it's important to find their answers. Confronting ourselves about the way we are living our lives is healthy. It is a path to leading a satisfying life. Unfortunately most people are too busy to see where their life is going. They are caught up in the complexities of work, family, and non-beneficial activities.

Focus first on how to please yourself. Ask yourself insightful questions. Don't let the barriers get in the way or inhibit future growth. Let it go. Move on to get ahead and use your strengths and capabilities to fulfill your purpose and work. It's time to renew yourself, your whole self, including both your professional side and your personal life. Spend more time thinking about *you*. I think we all should do this once each year. A scheduled time for most of us works; it isn't selfish. Get away to be alone with your thoughts. Time alone will help focus priorities and reestablish purpose.

Why Care for Yourself?
— *You Can Help Others*

Change or refresh your plan, and then initiate your changes. Your changing behaviors will influence others. These persistent actions require courage, both to implement them and to sustain the changes. Take it slow. Take some risks. You will quickly learn that the changes you make and actions you take have positive consequences. If you are doing the right things for the right reasons, you will have the confidence to confront the barriers standing in the way of your progress. I find with many of my coaching clients that the most difficult issues they face are within themselves. Courage is generated when you realize you are expressing your values and desire to live a purposeful life, as well as being very productive in your work.

The need to take care of yourself in order to take care of others the way you want to care for them is fundamental. If you aren't right with yourself, you may dilute your purpose and effectiveness for caring for your family and your coworkers. Your purpose will always include growing your care, love, and support for your family. You can reduce the effectiveness of your family care by not caring first for *you*. Your personal well-being must be a priority in your life. Be a bit selfish; first get in shape and on course before changing the focus of your priorities. You'll surprise yourself when you see that life gets better for others when you feel great. You will have more energy to help others, along with a new confidence that you will be ready to help when help is needed.

— *You Can Be Healthy*

Speed and busyness will eventually impact your immune system. You get sick. You and others around you may frequently get colds or be unwell in some way. You may eventually develop heart disease, high blood pressure, and other stress-related conditions. You may even need mental health care. Actually, being hospitalized may slow you down enough to save your life. Some of the worst cases of out-of-control speed and busyness addicts are still walking around, "infecting" others until they suddenly drop dead.

A forty-one-year-old client of mine insisted on remaining in a highly stressful and toxic environment. One day, after I hadn't heard from him for two months, he announced that he had acquired shingles. This is a virus that typically affects people over fifty. Stress in younger people creates conditions that foster it. Of course, there are many other reasons people catch shingles, including from other infected people—it's contagious—but stress was the reason in his case.

We've all heard that many people retire and then die not too long after they stop working. But retired people all tend to live longer if they have purpose in their life. An article in a 2008 issue of AARP magazine titled "Find Purpose, Live Longer"[12] suggests that having a purpose adds years to your life. "Today, at 104, Marge Jetton says she owes her can-do vitality to her religious faith and her fervid belief that as long as she's around, she can make a difference. A growing body of research suggests she may be onto something. A 2005 study that followed 12,640 middle-age Hungarians found that those who felt their lives had meaning had much lower rates of cancer and heart disease than did those who didn't feel this way. Another study of some of the world's most long-lived people, the Blue Zones project, discovered that "having a sense of purpose—or 'having a reason to get out of bed' was a common trait in many of the world's centenarians."

"People who feel their life is part of a larger plan and are guided by their spiritual values have stronger immune systems, lower blood pressure, a lower risk of heart attack and cancer, and heal faster and live longer," says Harold G. Koenig, MD,[13] professor of psychiatry and behavioral sciences at Duke University Medical Center, who has studied the phenomenon broadly. We not only live longer with purpose in our lives, we live a more satisfying life.

Get help when you are too out of control or when you don't think you can slow down. Feeling that you must be busy all of the time can become

---

12   Buettner, Dan, "Find Purpose, Live Longer," Mind and Body, *AARP the Magazine*, November/December 2008, Page 32.

13   Ibid.

compulsive behavior, harmful to your health. Seek out professionals who will help you slow down to a healthy pace. You may not be able to stop the downward spiral on your own. Find a confidant, coach, mentor, or therapist to help you regain a healthy perspective about the speed at which you live. You probably aren't being as productive as you think. You may break down, burn out, or get sick. Listen to what may be happening to your body. Your system initiates defensive reactions to the stress and chemical imbalances you create with a compulsive obsession to stay busy all of the time.

In *Toxic Success,* Paul Pearsall[14] describes the physical impact of stress responses. "To help you understand more about the fight-or-flight stress response associated with TSS, toxic stress syndrome, consider the following list of the body's stress reactions. Notice how the fight-or-flight stress reaction worked fine for fighting, hunting, killing, and outrunning a predator trying to eat us but has now become *what is eating us."* Pearsall goes on to provide details of the primitive benefits and current liability of the following physical and chemical changes in our bodies when under stress.

1. Hormonal surges

2. Thyroid pumping

3. Endorphin pumping

4. Sex hormone dipping

5. Digestive shutdown

6. Sugar high

7. Cholesterol flows

8. Heart races

9. Hyperventilating

10. Thickening of the blood

11. Goosebumps and sweat

12. All five senses heightened

---

14   Pearsall, Paul, PhD. *Toxic Success, How to Stop Striving and Start Thriving,* Ocean Publishing, Inc, 2002.

Get help when you notice that you are out of control. Feeling that you must be busy all of the time can become compulsive behavior and harmful to your health.

How to Care for Yourself

Start by slowing down. Assess the stress in your life and the environment you yourself may be creating. Take a broad view first; ask those important questions, and reassess your physical health and your strengths and weaknesses. Next, focus on the following areas to regain your health.

– *Eat Right*

The healthy foods you eat are a fast way to feel better. Be cautious about overeating: it slows you down in the wrong way. Besides the extra calories, overeating makes you sluggish. Digestion takes longer before you start feeling the energy from the food. You've noticed how it's difficult to reengage at work after a big lunch. The same is true in the evening at home with family. You will find more energy to accomplish your tasks and goals at home if you eat smaller portion. Slowing down to take care of yourself in order to "run faster" may seem counterintuitive, but this is what this entire book is helping you understand. Caring for your health needs to *always* be a priority in your life.

– *Get Fit*

Being physically fit is the next priority. Write your plan to get fit. Yes, write it down. I believe that this is a good reason why Weight Watchers is one of the most successful lifestyle weight loss programs. Recording goals and weekly activities to achieve those goals has a proven track record. I know that you have experienced this at some time in your life. Consider the following physical goals:

I want to weigh____by_____.

I want to lose____pounds a week.

I want to get____hours sleep each night.

I want to get a fitness coach to set up a program by_____.

I want to be fit enough to achieve _____by_____.

I will exercise effectively _____times a week for _____hour or minutes each day.

I will achieve a resting heart rate of_____pulses per minute by_____.

I will eat _____for the next _____weeks.

I will stop drinking alcohol or limit my drinking to_____for_____ weeks.

I will seek help and stop smoking by_____.

As always, check with your physician before starting any rigorous physical fitness program.

Reaching these goals will provide the energy and confidence necessary for you to perform better, get more done, and spend more time on your other priorities.

— *Sleep Enough*

You may think you have conditioned yourself to sleeping less than eight hours a night. Most people need seven to eight hours of sleep to renew the body. Please test yourself or speak with your physician about how much sleep you need. I have tested myself by getting eight hours of sleep each night for ten nights and journaling the positive and negative impacts. I find that I get out of bed easier, want to get started sooner, look forward to my first cup of coffee and checking out the weather outlook, and want to prioritize my day's activities early on. I have more energy in the early afternoon, and I'm more active after dinner. You may find that your attitude, energy level, outlook, sense of well-being or ability to get more done improve. I found that going from six hours of sleep to seven and a half hours of sleep a night had a positive impact on my energy level. I think it even helped my immune system, but only time will tell.

Thomas, a coaching client of mine, was skeptical of my suggestion to get more than six and a half hours of sleep a night. He said that he didn't need more, and he functioned well with between six and six and a half hours of sleep each night. I encouraged him to add a half hour of sleep each night for a week and see how he felt. He felt a little better, so I asked him to add another half hour over the next two weeks. He became a believer when he realized that he had more energy. He hired a fitness coach, and they worked out at 5:30 a.m. for two mornings a week. He also realized that he didn't have to work so late after the children went to bed. He got more work done at the office instead of taking work home because he was more productive. Thomas now gets seven and a half to eight hours of sleep each night and feels great.

Be careful of the stories you tell yourself about the amount of sleep that is sufficient for you, as Thomas did. You won't know how much better you'll feel until you change your sleep patterns. By the way, naps are very helpful as well.

– *Consider Your Spiritual Fitness*

Spiritual enrichment also needs to be considered a part of your emotional health and purpose plan for taking care of yourself. Is your spiritual life important to you? I ask every coaching client to confront this question. I personally believe that your spiritual growth usually needs your attention. Spiritual fitness can give you access to power, as well as comfort and peace. It's perfectly appropriate to question whether a spiritual life is genuinely important. These types of explorations are healthy, no matter the outcome. Even considering whether there is a God is a healthy question to ask. My personal and client experience is that clearing up ideas, suspicions, assumptions, disappointments, and disillusions can help you better understand your reality. It helps you break through emotional barriers that hold you back from fulfilling the life you want to lead. You can then accept your decisions with clarity and purpose.

— *Don't Overcommit*

As a whole person, you need enough energy to help yourself and others at home and at work. Be cautious about wasting your energy. Overcommitting is a frequent problem in busy lives and is a primary reason for wasting energy. You must deal with overload in order to have the energy to stick with priorities and fulfill objectives. How do you stop being overcommitted? There are probably many ways to do this diplomatically in the workplace without being insubordinate. Isn't this what worries you most? You have opportunities, even an obligation, to ask the uncomfortable questions of others at work. These questions may reveal wasted efforts, out of sync directions or activities, and counterproductive projects or changes. Some of what is expected of you can be overwhelming. You can choose to talk with others to help you understand and then decide whether the expectation is right for you and the organization. You can influence the direction of efforts or how work gets done by stepping up and asking for clarification. Make the choice to do what's right for you and others, for the sake of the business.

If we frequently overcommit, we place a great deal of stress on ourselves, and possibly others with whom we work. We can also be guilty of *not* keeping our commitments if we can't do what we said we could do. My clients realize how important it is to *not* overcommit when I tell them that overcommitting may negatively impact your integrity. If we don't behave with integrity we are not trusted. If we aren't trusted, we have little or no credibility. When I describe this impact to them, some clients slap their forehead and say "I never realized that not meeting my commitments had such a bad impact on my reputation." It does. Don't overcommit!

Overcommitting, of course, occurs in our personal lives. Young children in the family require a great deal of attention. School, studies, play, sports, etc., for their development takes time. Parents and single adults are involved with community, church, exercise, friends, home maintenance, etc. We need to make sure we are working on our priorities and focus on fulfilling our plans to take care of ourselves and our families.

– *Show Up As You*

Knowing what you stand for and demonstrating that every day means showing up as an authentic person. This attitude powerfully and positively influences you toward accomplishing what you want to do. You make better decisions, build confidence, take action, and achieve results just by demonstrating the person you really are. You will make choices that will make a difference in your life and work. Slowing down helps you make those choices.

I have asked executives these questions to demonstrate my point. Think of your best and most passionate employees or associates. How much time do you need to spend with them about the work they do? Every executive has responded with the same answer: "I manage them very little." For this and other reasons I suggest you focus on your strengths; they are your passions. Also, taking care of yourself is demonstrated by living and working in your passion.

– *Take "Alone Time"*

Periodically, your plan needs to be recalibrated. Make time to be alone with your thoughts, reveal what is in your heart, and open up to reset your priorities. This will allow you to see possibilities that you may have missed. It may be helpful to write down or journal your thoughts, feelings, and ideas. This will help clear your mind as you sort your thoughts.

Making time to be alone is important in caring for you. I call it "alone time." Slowing down your thoughts and activities is not wasting your time, although most Americans think that they always need to be busy. Alone time is a meaningful period for sorting out your thoughts and to question the value of activities. It may help you assess how you are living life. It will help you develop a healthy perspective about all the busyness and activities that surround you. It's a time to plan and renew your intentions in order to remain focused on the right priorities.

Schedule a regular time for removing yourself from the rest of the world to reflect on your purpose and mission and the commitments you have made to yourself. Consider the purposeful actions you'd like to take. Centering yourself quietly can mentally and emotionally program your intentions. This is a meditative activity. I call it "just being." Slowing down like this can get you further ahead because you can discover ideas generated in your heart and mind. Your subconscious will take over to automatically guide your actions toward fulfilling your mission or desired outcomes.

— *Put Your Strengths and Weaknesses into Perspective*

It's my experience while coaching clients that strengthening a weakness expends a great deal of energy and only improves the weakness to mediocre levels. As far as weaknesses are concerned, identify only those behaviors that are significant barriers to moving forward. I will never be a good golfer. I have thought about quitting the game altogether, even though golfing is a great way to spend time with my wife and friends. So I will play and hold off on my decision to give my clubs away. I've decided not to take myself so seriously and to enjoy the people with whom I share the course.

You should only attempt to improve one or two weaknesses at one time. Keep your expectations realistic. Remember that developing weaknesses will not improve them to be great. The easiest method of improving some behaviors is to simply stop doing them. Consider this option. Of course, some behaviors need to be improved, not ignored. By continuously developing yourself you show up as the unique person you are. By demonstrating your best attributes, you perform at your best. It is worth your time to slow down and write a development plan for yourself. Balance expanding your strengths with improving your weaknesses.

Are you doing things you hate to do? Or things you don't have the appetite or skills for? You may want to stop doing those activities. Let go of trying to get better at the activities and professional tasks you don't like to do. If you can, hire someone or delegate those activities. Assign work to others that you don't like or are not skilled at doing. Care about yourself by focusing on the passions that will enable you to grow faster because you have the positive energy to develop them. You will perform better when you develop in this way.

– Don't Forget to Dream

You need to dream and pursue your dreams. The busyness of life gets in the way of dreaming and planning and pursuing dreams. The dreams you dream are not always for yourself but include your family, friends, and business. Your dreams need to become part of your purpose and focus if you are serious about making the dreams become reality. Dream the possibilities, your hopes for the future. Being too busy to think and plan for what you want is denying yourself the possibilities of reaching your potential. Think about your potential by designing your future with intention. Live your potential. Don't waste the opportunity to do whatever you want to do with your life.

– Forgive Yourself

Forgive yourself or ask for forgiveness for the things left undone or the paths you may have taken in the wrong direction. Don't get stuck in the past. Understand that the life you led in the past had its reasons at the time. You didn't know what you now know. You may be seeking a different kind of life, lifestyle, or work. You can't forget the past, but you can see it with a different perspective. If appropriate, forgive yourself and let go of the baggage you may be dragging along behind you. Some of my clients call it "a bag of crap." Let go of it and move on. *Honor what you have learned from your past and pursue your purpose for the next chapter of your life.*

Forgiving yourself is a way of renewing your purpose and placing your energy in a positive and productive mode. Renewal is a way of focusing energy in the right direction and not wasting time, talent, and resources on the less important activities that don't move you closer to accomplishing your dreams. Spend your time on meaningful activities that are productive. Slowing down and renewing your mission is a productive activity because it identifies priorities and stops the busyness that is sucking energy away from your intended direction and outcomes. Refocusing on purpose reduces chances of moving in an unintended direction.

– Ask for Help

A professor of philosophy stood before his class with some items in front of him. When the class began, he picked up a large empty mayonnaise jar and proceeded to fill it with rocks about two inches in diameter. He then asked the students if the jar was full. They agreed that it was full.

The professor then picked up a box of pebbles and poured them into the jar. He watched as the pebbles rolled into the open areas between the rocks. The professor then asked the students again if the jar was full. They again agreed that it was full this time.

The professor picked up a box of sand and poured it into the jar. The sand filled the remaining space in the jar.

The professor said, "Now, I want you to recognize that this jar signifies your life. The rocks are the truly important things, such as family, health, and relationships. If all else was lost and only the rocks remained, your life would still be meaningful. The pebbles are the other things that matter in your life, such as work or school. The sand signifies the remaining 'small stuff' and material possessions.

"If you put the sand into the jar first, there is no room for the pebbles, and the rocks. The same goes for your life. If you spend all your energy and time on the small stuff, you will never have room for the things that are important to you. Pay attention to the things that are critical to your happiness. Play with your children. Take time to get medical checkups. Take your wife out dancing. There will always be time to go to work, clean the house, give a dinner party, and fix the disposal."

Take care of the rocks first—the things that really matter. Set your priorities. The rest is just sand.[15]

While pursuing what is right for you in your personal care, as well as the care of others, slowing down to make choices and refocus is very helpful and healthy. Sharing yourself with others is something most people want to do. You probably receive a warm feeling when helping others grow or perform well. Find the time to control activities that create a chaotic work environment and focus on the priorities that are important to the mission. The quality of your personal life is also determined by the priorities you choose to attend to. The story above illustrates this point.

By allowing useless activities and busyness to fill your days, you lose control. Slow down and get back to controlling what you can control. You can ask for help if you are stuck or really don't know how to get back

---

15 Covey, Stephen R., Merrill, A. Roger, and Merrill, Rebecca R., *First Things First,* Simon and Schuster, 1994.

in control. Asking for help is a mature thing to do when you are out of control or caught up in the unproductive busyness. Most of the time it's ego that inhibits asking for help. You think you are supposed to have all the answers. You may assume that asking for help is a sign of weakness. In the business environment, it's frequently arrogance within the company culture that keeps you from asking for help. You can't know everything. Asking for help is asking for information, knowledge, experience, and wisdom from other people who surround you. Arrogance merely blocks facing the truth and reality of the situation. The sooner you see the truth, the sooner you can take corrective actions. Any other action slows the work down. Get help as soon as possible.

– *Clear Up Assumptions*

Assumptions are another form of disillusionment that creep into daily life and inhibit choices and actions. We frequently live with these assumptions; they become the stories we tell ourselves. The stories may not be reality. Assumptions are just guesses, but you make judgments based on those guesses. Clear up assumptions as soon as they start creeping into your thoughts. Take action to go to the source and ask some simple questions. Express what is going through your mind and let others know you want to understand what's real. Don't waste your energy thinking or steaming about an assumption. You create too much useless baggage and waste emotional energy. It is so much easier to move ahead, unencumbered by the stories we may be making up. You may be making inaccurate judgments about situations and people. Confronting your stories allows you to create more powerful stories that are based on truth and reality.

Frequently you may be silent about the demands placed on you. That's when you allow yourself to get overcommitted. I know it may seem easy for me to say that you are obligated to stand up and speak out or ask the obvious question that many others won't ask. I've helped many people overcome this fear; they then realize that the work environment improves when they engage in dialogue in a healthy and respectful manner. This dialogue clears up assumptions. Clear your mind and emotions by respectfully taking action. You will be helping others as well as yourself if you step up and act.

Take Care of Others
— *Those in Your Family*

A friend of mine had many businesses in the first half of his adult life. His family was neglected by his busyness and need to succeed. After a divorce he wanted to reconcile with his children in order to establish a good relationship with them. He was able to reestablish a relationship with three of his children after awhile. But his oldest daughter told him that all he was to her was a sperm donor, nothing more.

We need to look around at how our family is doing—I mean *really* doing. If you've been out of control and highly stressed for a long period of time, your family will have made many adjustments for their own preservation. We need to look deeply into the impact of our business life and the speed at which we live. A great deal has been written about this stressful way of living and working. Stop to listen to what is going on with family members. You need to slow down to talk with them to learn more about what they are doing, the issues they deal with, and what experiences they are having. Ask about what they think of you. Do they need more from you?

— *Extended Family*

Extended family is also another consideration in maintaining and enriching relations. The importance of your extended family is something you need to establish before you spend your efforts building or rebuilding relations. You must want to do so. Realize that this may be a choice, not a responsibility. Be clear with your own intentions. Some extended families are very close, and some are distant and grow more distant with life and time.

If enriching the relations with your extended family is important to you, do something to grow the relationships. If it isn't important, just maintain the current relationships.

— *Don't Fool Yourself*

Workaholics are the contrast to how we'd prefer to live our life. They think that they are working hard in order to take care of the family and provide for a better life. Workaholics are lying to themselves and others.

Their condition can be an addiction. They can be compulsive about work and achievement. We can all work very hard for long hours from time to time. When the work becomes an end in itself, the individual has become a workaholic.

John O'Neil, in his book *The Paradox of Success*,[16] writes about "Performance Addiction." He says, "As the growing literature devoted to stress and burnout shows, high performance has its shadow side. Workaholism is now seen as an addiction, a pattern of compulsive behavior—good things pushed to the point of abuse." This type of behavior may mean that workaholics merely focus on themselves and don't consider family needs. Paul Pearsall, in *Toxic Success,* provides a definition of *self-sightedness*: "Constant distraction and self-focus resulting in what psychologists call "inattentive blindness" to the most important things and people in our life."

The questions to ask are:

- Is the hard worker working for him- or herself or the family?

- Does the family need the things that the workaholic is striving to buy or create?

- Who's working for whom?

There needs to be clarity around the reasons for working long hours. I know that the economic crises and downsizing may have you performing the work of two or three people. The reasons for the hard work must be understood by your spouse and possibly the entire family. Pearsall also points out that relationship exploitation may be occurring. This is "neglect, usury, and abuse of our most intimate relationships by taking them for granted, using them only as safe havens from stress, a quick intimacy fix, or a stress-reduction technique."

- What are the priorities?

- What is the ultimate purpose of family and work?

---

16 O'Neil, John, *The Paradox of Success*, Jeremy P. Tracher/Putnum, member of Penguin Putman, Inc. 1993.

You can miss out on a great deal of life if you don't slow down and truly understand why you spend so much time working. You can rationalize your way into missing out on the experiences of your children: precious moments that can never be recaptured.

Validate the values, agreements, and commitments that are important to you by discussing them with your family. Open up the conversation by discussing your thoughts and then listen to what others have to say. Listen for the insights into what's important to others. Keep in mind that what they first say may not be what they really mean when you first approach the topic; probe for truth and reality. If you proceed in this manner, you will be sharing love just by asking them what's really important to them. Don't underestimate the power of asking such questions and discussing how they shape each family member's priorities. People are all in a different place at any point in time. Slow down to talk individually, as well as a family group. At first they may not want to share their feelings. They may need to process their thoughts and feelings for a time. They may also be caught up in the busyness of *their* worlds. Do whatever it takes to hold these important discussions. These conversations may turn out to be among those precious events you want to embrace, remember, and repeat in the future.

Everyone has important thoughts, plans, and feelings. Show you recognize their importance just by asking questions about what they want. They will also ask you questions that may make you feel uncomfortable. That's great! Get uncomfortable. Confront the issues that exist. And it's okay if you don't have all the answers. Unanswered questions are an opportunity to work together. Questions from your children will help you understand what your family cares about.

— *Your Friends*

Take care of your friends. Be there for fun and sharing life. As you grow into your fifties, sixties, seventies, eighties, and nineties, you'll find you actually value friendship more than at any other time of your life. Children are usually grown by then or at least more on their own. They don't need you as much as they used to. You are looking for more out of life in your fifties. This is usually the time when many people move into a new chapter of life. Friends can become another focus of attention. Typically, friendships have more meaning as you age.

Other things become important as you move into your sixties. Grandchildren are probably in your life by this time. This is another opportunity to revisit the "family" purpose plan. There are other things to consider in the sixties, such as: retirement, financial stability, saving for the future, working into another cycle of your career, having new adventures, and, of course, taking your grandchildren to Disney World. There are more reasons at this age to slow down and plan again. Create another vision of what you want for the *growing* family and your future.

Those in Your Business
— *Work Impact*

Your work environment can also suffer if you are out of control with busyness, always being connected to your smart phone and checking things off of your To Do list. You probably expect the same from the people who report to you. You then become toxic to them and the rest of the work environment. You are then considered a virus, and other people get sick along with you. The business eventually suffers. You and your subordinates are not as productive in meeting expectations; results become diluted or quality of outcomes declines. You and your team may fall short of the expectations of senior management. I've seen this occur many times.

Morale in the American workforce is dropping very quickly in companies that don't recognize that too much of "doing more with less" can break down the enthusiasm of the people and drive them into busyness and just not caring about the quality of what they do. Western business cultures may be heading in the wrong direction. This is already being reflected in how difficult it is to retain good talent. The speed of change and the way we lead the workforce isn't allowing us to spend sufficient time with each person in order to properly listen to them and explore their ideas, thoughts, and desires regarding their growing career. The war for talent is going to become worse. Younger generations want to make a difference by having input into the way work gets done. They want a voice.

Success Factors website shares the *Performance & Talent Management Trends Survey 2007,* which states, "America's largest 500 companies will lose 50 percent of their senior managers in the next five years, according to RHR International. And a survey by the Society for Human Resource Management said that 83 percent of workers were likely to search for a new job in the coming couple of years."[17]

We need baby boomers to continue working, contributing, and doing meaningful work, not just putting in the hours. Older workers may teach us how to better lead and manage a workforce that listens to people in their twenties and thirties. Most in the traditional and baby boomer generations don't really need the money. They can easily walk away from their jobs, although the 2008 financial crisis kept baby boomers working longer. I suggest that they will take more risks with their bosses and stand up to tell them their thoughts and push back on leaders. The 2011 financial crisis is compounding the issues for effectively managing and keeping talented people.

We may learn a great deal over the next ten years that will help us better lead people and improve the work environment for the American worker.

Time to Pause

What are the three things you want to do to be in better shape and take care of yourself?

What spiritual needs are missing in your life?

While reviewing your priorities, what two or three activities can you let go of and not do?

What is the most important issue you need to face and push back on?

Talk with each member of your family alone. Ask your questions and answer theirs.

---

17 "Performance and Talent Management Trends Survey," Success Factors Web site, http://www.successfactors.com/articles/performance-management-trends/2007.

Part III:
Planning Purpose and Action

7

Rediscover Who You Are

Determine Who You Are

Family is usually the most important part of your life. Work frequently comes second. Various parts of your life are more important than others. But life is driven by the people you love and the things you love to do. Love is a universal value that most people can understand and embrace. I've ask many of my friends and colleagues what they thought was a value that anyone in the world could hold dear to them. The only value that seems to be universal is *love*. We need to receive it, and we need to give it. Love for family and others is fundamental to a meaningful life.

Values and Beliefs

Be aware of your capabilities. Look ahead as far as you can reasonably see into the future: plan your life to that point. Don't plan for the rest of your life. Conditions are changing too frequently. Awareness of your capabilities, values, and beliefs will provide the foundation for stabilizing the most important part of your life: what you want for you and your family. We want our children to grow with a good education and with our love and guidance and have experiences that will help them be responsible and contributing members of society. These values and beliefs will not change very much, if at all.

We can only find real satisfaction by living a value-based life, by planning our life and work around what we value most. Richard Leider, in his book *The Power of Purpose*[18], states, "The integration of who you are with what you do is one of the true joys in life. You're all challenged to shape and create the specific and unique way you are going to do the work you are called to do. Discovering your calling means living your values. It means putting your values to work by resolving to make what you do reflect who you really are."

Start with some important questions to identify your values, explore new directions, and understand what barriers are in your way.

- What values do I have and embrace in my personal and professional life?
- Which of my behaviors conflict with my value system?
- What am I doing on this treadmill that I need to stop doing?
- How can I focus on doing the right things and stop or change doing the wrong things in my personal and professional life?
- What value or contribution am I making to fulfill my purpose and professional mission?

The answers to these questions will help you start making changes in the way you live. Reflect on what is going on in your life. Don't get caught up in the stories that take away from your purpose and mission.

- What do you appreciate?
- Who is really important to you?
- Are you doing what you love to do?
- What is giving you pain?

---

18 Leider, Richard J., *The Power of Purpose*, Barrett-Koehler Publishing, Inc., 1997.

- Are you dealing with the issues that confront you?

Answers to these questions become the stories you tell yourself. The stories you develop describe the way you're living your life. If you tell yourself that something is important, it's important. If you tell yourself that something is right, it's right. If you ignore a truth or facts, you deceive yourself. We all make many assumptions about what is going on around us. Clearing your assumptions reduces the stories that you make up without having any facts to support them.

- Why do I feel the way I do about my life and work?
- What am I assuming about my future?
- Do I really have control over the outcomes or does someone else?
- Am I letting life just happen to me?
- Am I working for something that I really want?
- Am I living an enriching life or do I feel empty and shallow?

These questions can clarify whether you are living with made-up stories or the truth. Clear your thoughts; as you do, you open up new directions and possibilities. This is an opportunity to make a correction in your life. Don't wait; do it as soon as possible. You may want to ask others to help you clear up your assumptions. Get some help and get centered again.

The Best You

Rediscover the best you. The best you is when you are using your God-given talents and gifts. Richard Leider writes in *The Power of Purpose:*[19] "We each possess gifts and valuable talents. This fundamental assumption has proved true for everyone whom I have coached over the past twenty years. Everyone is gifted in some way. Many of us might deny that this is the case simply because we have never focused on our strengths; rather, we have focused on our weaknesses." Leider goes on to say, "We all have

---

19 Leider, *The Power of Purpose.*

natural abilities and inclinations and find that certain things come easily to us. We may perform a talent so effortlessly that we forget we have it. This is a "gift." Focusing on using your gifts will lead you to becoming your best."

Based on my own coaching clients, I concur with Leider's experiences. Be authentic. The process of discovering or realizing who you are and what you stand for helps bring into focus what is most important to pursue in your next chapter of life and work. Bring out the real you. Living life around strengths, purpose, and passions is powerful and energizing. Experience the adventure within. Living from strengths can be stabilizing. Eliminate possible paths that could prove unproductive or impractical. When you focus on what you really want you will save energy, be clear when opportunities pop up, and decrease distractions that are not right for you and your family.

Personal and Professional Alignment

Conflict between the way we live our personal and professional lives is unhealthy. Have you heard coworkers say, "I don't take work home with me" or "I don't talk about work with my spouse"? I believe that few of us can really keep work and home separate in a healthy way. Most of us have trouble with this philosophy and are actually fooling ourselves most of the time. How can I be the authentic me if I behave one way at home and another way at work? This way of living adds stress to an already stressful life. Some people may think that they are saving their family from the sinister behaviors they may exhibit at work, but they are living two different lives. If this resonates with you, there's something wrong. What is it? Are you working in a toxic environment that wants you to behave in a way that isn't really you or your natural behavior? Are you infecting others with this behavior as well?

Plan your personal life and professional career to express the same values, purpose, and passions. Integrate values with the way you want to live. Having a plan for yourself will help you control what you can control in life and work. It will help you make good choices on a daily basis. Make choices about how you treat others at work; collaborate with others to solve a problem. Respect the views of others while moving ahead to accomplish your purpose or mission. Don't let work behaviors and various personal behaviors get in the way of working together to accomplish the goals of your organization. Execute your plans by being honest, straightforward, and passionate.

Conflict within us is demonstrated through our demeanor. We can't really hide this conflict very long. It can show up as depression or some other disorder. Please be cautious about fooling yourself. Take time to slow down and take a good look at yourself as you plan your life and work. Then you will be moving toward a healthy, rewarding, and satisfying life.

Identifying these conflicts or core issues takes time and thoughtful reflection and may require getting help. Slow down and seek the truth. You must get away from it all in order to really think about what is important to you. I don't mean taking a restful vacation with the family. I mean spending deliberate time alone. There are organizations that can help people work through the reflective process. Consider that option if life is so busy that you don't know how to slow down on your own.

External Forces

Many times events out of your control force you to make different choices about what you do for work, what you need to learn, and what you require in order to grow differently than you have in the past. Remember the hull and keel of your sailboat as described in the Life Control Model. Your foundation of values and beliefs will help you make those choices that may take you in new directions.

A great example of events beyond our control is the global financial crises. Fear blanketed us. We didn't know what to do. Some people froze. Some people got out of the stock market. Some stayed in. Many people lost their jobs and later their homes. Governments around the world tried to react quickly with monetary funds, new financial policies, and strategies for protecting home owners. Global financial economists started to rethink how banking and the financial markets operate and how they need to change.

During these crises, families reacted by making important choices for themselves. They started spending money differently, purchasing only the essentials: making lunches to take to work, limiting driving, buying less expensive goods, and saving what they could. Think about how you reacted and the choices you made. What actions did you take that were within your control? No matter what you did, this was the time to stand on your values.

"I need to do what I can to care for my family by ..."
"I need to work with my colleagues to get us through this crisis."
"I need to do everything I can to keep my job secure."
"I need to pray about the situation and ask for guidance."
"I need to think about others who may be impacted by ___"
"I need to get back to the basics of what's important in my life."
"What else can I do to utilize my talents and make a living?"
"I need to find a new career."

External events forced you to make choices and take actions to adjust your lifestyle to survive, sustain, and thrive. In many ways the 9/08 and 2011 financial crises changed our lives permanently. The event was out of our control, but the choices we made were within our control.

Strength in Talents

Developing strengths or using existing strengths to make a better life for yourself can make a big difference toward getting what you want. Find something within this new chapter that fits your natural talents. This does *not* mean that your past experiences are your strengths. People can be in the wrong job for years, not using their strongest talents. Leverage fundamental, God-given gifts to use in the next chapter of your life.

Talent is frequently described as a special natural ability or aptitude. Objective views of strengths and natural talents are helpful during this discovery process. Assessments are an objective way to find out who you are and what your hidden talents are. Consider taking a Meyers-Briggs, DISC, Strong Preference, Extended DISC, Birkman, Change Grid, or other assessment. Most of these are inexpensive to take and include a professional interpretation of the results. Clients who take an assessment report that they are fairly accurate, and they rarely disagree with the results. Many didn't realize that they haven't been using all of their talents.

The Gallup Organization interviewed two million people to determine that it's more important to focus on developing your strengths than your weaknesses. Marcus Buckingham and Donald O. Clifton, PhD, of Gallup coauthored the book *Now, Discover Your Strengths.*[20] They write, "You will excel only by maximizing your strengths, never by fixing your weaknesses. This is not the same as saying, "Ignore your weaknesses." The people we described did not ignore their weaknesses. Instead, they did something much more effective. They found ways to manage around their weaknesses, thereby freeing them up to hone their strengths to a sharper point." The book leads you to the Strengths Finder Profile. This is an excellent way of identifying your natural talents. I suggest you identify your God-given talents; they are your strengths. These strengths are usually demonstrated in what you really love to do. These things are your "sand box."

The results of this and other exercises to identify strengths can confirm what we probably know about ourselves. We don't always consciously take action to develop our strengths or use them in the work we do. We also keep trying to improve our weaknesses. My earlier suggestion was to get someone else to do what you are not proficient in and do not want to do. This is a way of managing weaknesses. Don't spend much time worrying about weaknesses. Remember that if people work on correcting a behavior that they are weak in, they usually only develop it to a mediocre level. Focus more on taking your strengths to the next level.

Strength in Spiritual Values

The other element to consider is spiritual life and how it is integrated into your wholeness as a person. No matter what your religious preference, love is integrated into most religions and spiritual expressions.

Your spiritual life needs to be assessed when you are identifying how you want to live your life based on your values. Some people will deny their spiritual side, but there is reason to confront it from time to

---

20 Buckingham, Marcus and Clifton, Donald O., PhD, *Now Discover Your Strengths: The revolutionary program that shows you how to develop your unique talents and strengths—and those of the people you manage.* Free Press, 2001.

time. Rediscovering the power and peace in your spiritual side can have a wonderful impact on your life, forever.

How important is spirituality to you?

How long are you going to just let it go on the way it may be going?

What do you want to develop in your spiritual life?

What may you be missing by not having a closer relationship with God?

What are you in denial about?

How do your feelings and actions impact others around you by the way you address your spiritual life?

Ask yourself these reflective questions, and then take appropriate action if you think spiritual growth is important to your future. Your spiritual life may be a strength that can be used for the good of self and others. This may be a fundamental strength that has been buried or somehow lost. It may be easier to avoid these questions, but at least you can confront the importance of cultivating a spiritual life. Grow your spiritual life as a useful strength. Spirituality usually completes the wholeness in a person. Spiritual life may be a way of finding inner peace, being open to divine help in situations where there is no control, and providing some important answers to dilemmas in our lives.

Personal planning based on values, including spiritual values, provides the opportunity to move ahead and renew life, as well as work. I help clients be the same person at work as they are at home. When planning our personal life based on purpose and passions, we can also manage our professional life by using spiritual values as a foundation for both. We all find clarity when we are being realistic about ourselves, our capabilities, and how we can be at our best. Isn't this what we want to do—use our strengths?

Strength in Self-Awareness

In order to make confident choices, it is essential to be aware of values, strengths, and capabilities. Self-awareness is the place to start when moving into a new chapter of your life or work. The financial crisis may have led you into planning a new chapter for your life. Slow down to think about your "calling" or the next calling that is in you. Your personal life may be impacted by unfortunate events, such as financial downturns, illness, tragedy, loss, or divorce. Your company may have shut down, downsized, or merged with another company, or maybe it can't compete in the marketplace as it did in the past.

Investment banks folding and merging shook the financial stability of the United States and most other developed countries. Major events such as these impact everyone and are beyond our control. As I mentioned before, you are still the same person, with capabilities and values as your stable foundation. Make choices now as you enter a new chapter of life based on your capabilities, experiences, and values. Make some significant changes in your life and create an opportunity that may be better than your current situation. Although it may be difficult to look at the situation at first, be optimistic about the future.

Strength in Relationships

Relationships with others are important for growth and enrichment. The quality of relationships is the essence of who we are and what we want to share with others. The roles we play require that we develop many relationships. Investing time and energy in building and enriching relationships is rarely regretted. Therefore, relationship building is commonly included in purpose plans that take this strength to the next level.

Love is important and needs attention in order to receive it and give it in life. Of course, loving others involves building good relationships and spending time to enrich them. Careers need time to grow and be enriched, as well. We grow in our work by planning to learn what is needed and building the relationships to support it.

Be Aware that Your Brain May Deceive You

Our brains are filled with information, memories, programmed learning, and experiences. The cat only jumps on the hot stove once. It doesn't like stove tops after it's been burned. This is an experience that is programmed into the cat's brain. But most of the time the stove, a place where the cat can scrounge extra tidbits of food, is safe to touch. We have learned lessons in similar ways throughout our lives.

Most of the things that we learned at a young age are imprinted on our brain. We currently use the slang *hardwired* to describe this type of brain programming. We make our choices and take action based on the information stored in our brain.

The programmed nature of our brain can help us as well as limit our capability. Gunnar Nilsson, in his book *Human Bandwidth*,[21] tells us how our brain operates to help us day by day, as well as how our brain limits our ability to change. "Historically based, survival-oriented, habitual and repetitive, our minds reinforce unconscious habits and resist change. Perhaps as much as 80 percent of our thoughts are repetitive. These repetitive thoughts are primarily responsible for programming our behavior and actions. The voice inside our head keeps us locked in our habits and patterns. Our minds serve as a tour guide throughout the day. This repetitive programming robs each of us the creative, spontaneity, awareness, and human spirit inherent in our bandwidth because it takes us out of the present moment." He later goes on to say, "After a lifetime of conditioning, most of us come to believe that our internal voices are who we are. This false identity, forged in the mind, constantly asserts itself to remind us of who (we think) we are. High-volume thoughts and years of judging and criticizing ourselves have programmed us."

Our brain is an amazing and awesome organ. We are learning more about the brain each year. I believe we haven't given enough attention to the brain compared to the heart, liver, kidneys, and other vital organs. I think it is still a frontier for incredible exploration. I want to say that I have enormous respect for the complexity of the brain, even though I may at times criticize some of its functionality.

We are programmed by our genes, background, experiences, and development. The programming Nilsson describes happens by chance and learning. Of course, there is programming when our instincts take over, such as when we are frightened and flee from danger. Instincts protect us for continued survival.

---

21 Nilsson, Gunnar, *Human Bandwidth, Awakening the Extraordinary Within*, Rapid Creek Publishing, 2002.

Using Intuition

Because of this programmed brain conditioning, be careful of the lies your brain may be telling you; separate the programmed response from the truth. Ask yourself, "What is right for these times or situations?" Intuition will help balance the things we've learned in the past. It's a good filter for our consideration. Surely, intuition is the natural side of human beings. Trust your instincts first. Analyze all of the facts, as well as past experiences, but don't rely totally on facts alone. This may seem complex, but the process actually simplifies your decision-making process.

The Reader's Digest Great Encyclopedia Dictionary[22] describes intuition as "A direct knowledge or awareness of something without conscious attention or reasoning; nonintellectual perception or apprehension." Intuition is our ability to sense things around us. Most of us don't react or make decisions based on our intuition. Actually, intuition is a great asset that we could all benefit from exercising more. Balancing intuition with logic and our brain programming is the key to making good choices. Balancing these elements allows you to slow down and review your feelings as well as the information to make the best choices. Test your own decision-making preferences. Consider these questions:

- When I make major decisions, do I use more of my head (brain), body, gut (intuition), or spirit (heart)?

- How does using one more heavily than others affect the outcomes of my decisions?

- When I've used a mix of head, gut, and heart, what have the results been?

These are always curious questions. Mind, body, and spirit are the elements of good intuition.

The power of intuition is realized when you see into the future or can develop a realistic scenario for the actions you are about to take. You can visualize the future and have confidence that you can do what you want. Seeing into the future is not looking into a crystal ball. Intuition is a "sense" that what you want to do is right, and you can have confidence

---

22 Funk and Wagnalls, *Readers Digest Great Encyclopedia Dictionary*, Standard College Dictionary, 1968.

that you can successfully take the necessary actions. It allows you to listen to a variety of natural sources and balance them to make good decisions. You will bring your values, experience, learning, and feelings into play. Good choices include a combination of these elements, and most of us rarely use them all together.

Our mind needs to hold the right knowledge and experience to analyze and support action. Spirit provides the emotional energy to stay focused and carry us along the path of our actions. This combination is considered "intuition in play." It also represents for the breadth of possible choices. We can leverage this positive and powerful energy if we keep our thoughts, physical self, and feelings in balance.

The use of intuition in the business environment is expressed as "gut." Daniel Goleman and Richard Boyatzis said the following about the "Finely Attuned Leader" in their September 2008 *Harvard Business Review* article, "Social Intelligence and the Biology of Leadership."[23] "Great executives often talk about leading from the gut. Indeed, having good instincts is widely recognized as an advantage for a leader in any context, whether in reading the mood of one's organization or in conducting a delicate negotiation with the competition. Leadership scholars characterize this talent as an ability to recognize patterns, usually born of extensive experience. Their advice: Trust your gut, but get lots of input as you make decisions."

Choices and decisions are usually made quickly. Frequently we are rushed to make a choice during our work day. We are busy, and work won't get done until we make this decision. Hurry, hurry! We hurry when we need to slow down. Placing ourselves in "neutral" may often be difficult to do, because when we are rushed, our brain is programmed for an automatic response. Slowing down to think, discuss, and probe will get you to the core of the issue or opportunity and help you understand the reality of the situation. Take a deep breath, talk to others, and use intuition in order to avoid using a programmed, default response. Listening to your "inner voice"—intuition—rather than your programmed brain helps you determine right choices from wrong choices. First, listen to your intuition carefully. Examine how and what you feel. Ask questions about what is

---

23 Goleman, Daniel and Boyatzis, Richard, "Social Intelligence and the Biology of Leadership," *Harvard Business Review*, September 2008.

going on in your gut. Slow down to ensure you are making a values-based choice or decision. Then take action. Use these methods in both work and life decisions.

Balancing Your Brain, Intuition, and Heart

Balance your intuition and brain power. In his 1996 essay, "Decisions Using Intuition and Creativity,"[24] Robert J. Ballantyne wrote, "In this case I want to distinguish between craft and instinct. Anyone can learn about business plans, construction, etc., but without the instinctive ability to recognize a possibility, civilization will not move forward. I suspect that everyone shares parts of these instincts." He goes on to say, "The essence seems to be in the process of making decisions which result in action (or deliberate inaction). There seems to be a belief that decisions flow out of deliberate thought-processes. Both my current reading and my experience suggest that this is true."

Using instinct is a somewhat mysterious, but very useful, process in balancing the brain's normal thought-provoking, decision-making process; i.e. collecting information, collaborating, analyzing data, relying on past experiences, and thinking things out. Integrating intuition into traditional decision making brings creativity into the mix of possibilities.

Balance Intuition and Honesty

You will express your value judgment if you consistently show up as your authentic self. Credibility may be at stake. Honest and open expressions of doing the right thing will always serve you well. Political decisions may also be best served by using your intuitive instincts rather than a programmed response from your brain.

At times you may second-guess yourself or lose confidence because you may have lost your foundation for making the right choices. Be honest with yourself. Go back to your purpose and mission. Where are you really headed? Your core principles are embodied in the "hull of your sailboat." Slow down when in doubt. Review your principles. Rethink what is most important and what may be changing to impact your desires and

---

24   Ballantyne, Robert J., "Decisions Using Intuition and Creativity", an essay, July 3, 1996. http:/www.ballantyne.com/Intuition.html

outcomes. Now, assimilate the responses in your head, gut, heart, values, and purpose. You will be well equipped to make the best possible choices for yourself.

Balance Brain Power

There isn't a perfect formula for making the right choices; some risk is involved as you decide among various choices. You are striving to collect sufficient information, facts, and experience for you to be 80 percent to 90 percent confident in your decisions. As your experiences grow, you build the confidence needed to continue to make the right decisions. Keep in mind that the situations and experiences of the past may not fit the situation you currently face. What is important is that you slow down sufficiently to observe what facts have changed, what new resources are available, or what has changed in your personal and professional environment. Slow down enough to reevaluate the mental programming that worked for you in the past; add feelings, senses, insights, and integrity to the process. Listen to your intuitive voice, add the facts, and take action.

Balance Curiosity

Curiosity is a trigger that stimulates good questions that help you think through or process information to make a decision. Asking questions of yourself and others slows you down so you can separate facts from emotion, brain programs from intuition, and mission from non-important activities. Collaborating with others frequently starts with a key question or two.

Will this idea/action accelerate where we want to go?
Is this investment of resources worth pursuing?

Questions seem to breed more questions, but eventually you discover answers or solutions. Decide when enough questions are enough and just move ahead to a decision. You've made a decision, weighed the risks, and checked your intuition. You are 80 to 90 percent confident, so *move on.*

Curiosity is an important trait to develop. It not only slows you down enough to ask the important questions, but it also leads you to take a broader view of the situation. You may focus only on the narrow view unless you allow your curiosity to assess the situation from other perspectives and view points. You're able to explore additional possibilities that may lead you to better outcomes or enhance the results of your decisions. The broader view may also test what you have in your brain. Your brain usually focuses on past experiences and what you already know. Curiosity challenges what you know and explores other options or possibilities.

Balance Conflicting Feelings

At times we encounter inner conflict, when "things don't feel right." Something is wrong, and we don't know what it is. Listen to what is happening within your intuitive powers. Your brain and your intuition are in conflict. Analyze what is going on. It may be wise to delay making a decision. Walk away for a short time to let your intuition surface and allow your brain to assess your feeling that "This feels right!" or "Something is wrong." Explore what is wrong. Talk to others about how you feel. And don't try to justify that your brain is right. You may start rationalizing and accept that you, or your brain, are right without getting the input you need to make the right choices. Your intuition is an inner strength. Allow your intuition to guide you. When in great doubt, ask for help from others; ask for some spiritual guidance, and listen to it. When you sail your boat you assess the skies, wind speed, wind direction, and the waves before you adjust your direction. You must also feel the boat: wind resistance, pull on the sails, wind speed, yawl and pitch, and how your boat is moving through the waves. Sailing according to sense and feel assimilates a combination of facts, experiences, and intuitions so you can make choices in real time.

Consider your intuitive nature rather than your brain. Then let your brain continue by searching facts, objective analyses, resources, and past experiences. Remember that your brain can lie to you. Your intuition doesn't lie. It is the natural instinct that surfaces when you listen to what you sense and feel. Trust your intuition.

A conflict between the brain and intuition is actually a healthy occurrence. Conflicts are to be confronted, not suppressed. It's important to get the conflicts out on the table in the workplace as well as at home.

Deal with the truth and reality of the situation. Expose what is bothering loved ones and other people around you. They are probably exploring their instincts as well. Give them some time. It may take awhile for the intuitive pieces to surface and become clear.

Explore the possibilities collectively. We usually come up with a better path when others are asked to get involved in the best way to move ahead. To make good decisions, create synergy among all of the parts. Slowing down provides an opportunity to learn. Simply learning and seeking possibilities helps take us down the right path and realize our purpose and mission.

Balance Heart

Another way of approaching choices is to first "lead with your heart." Your intuition is connected to your heart. Your heart is a guide.

Where is your heart in all of this?
What do you really want?

We've heard these questions many times. We've asked others these questions. These are great questions that help you lead with your heart. Goodness, compassion, sensitivity, knowing right from wrong, and caring are all elements of the heart and the values that are in our heart and intuition—maybe even in our bloodstream.

Leading with heart will also stop you from selling out in situations that are in conflict with your values. You need to live with yourself. Heart is there to give us life and, I believe, to nurture the soul.

Time to Pause

Describe five strengths that you can develop to the next level.

Seek situations where you made a good decision by integrating your brain power, heart, and intuition. Now use these elements to decide about something in your future.

Tonight, with your spouse, family member, or friend, ask a thought-provoking, open-ended question and then listen for a deeper meaning in what they said. Be very quiet, and don't interrupt. Use your intuition to form other questions to get to the essence of the response. Articulate your discovery.

Consider a situation you are currently struggling with. What are your feelings about the situation, and how does this impact you? *First*, use your intuition to find a response. *Then* look at the facts. Test your responses with someone else.

8
How to Plan

Having a plan is an important first step in taking charge of your life and career. If you don't have a plan, you won't know where you want to go, and you will settle for any outcome. Your desired results will only occur when you take control, so start figuring out where you want to go and create a written plan. You do need to write your plan down. The planning process is similar to setting goals. Spend thoughtful time to ensure that your goals are right for you throughout the planning process.

Plan Your Personal Life First

You have answered the important questions in previous chapters. You have also started your planning process. Let's explore some ways to design the next chapter of your life, starting with what you want for your family and yourself. I'll ask more questions about what you want in the next three to five years, a chapter in your life. Jot down your answers in the book or in your notebook.

Continuous change is a condition we will face for the rest of our lives. We need to know how to manage this fast-changing environment we live and work in or suffer the stress of the changes. We no longer live our lives in a linear fashion. We live our lives in chapters. Chapters are an important concept for managing change. For example, rarely will your purpose and future planning be a lifelong plan. A chapter in your life may only last between two and five years. Something usually occurs that upsets longer-term plans, such as the 9/08 financial crisis. Some colleagues of mine think that changing careers may become as common as changing jobs.

Chapters versus Purpose

There are times when we confuse our chapter goals and purpose with our lifetime goals. Chapter goals will change as necessary when our environment changes. Lifetime goals are what we want in our life for the rest of our life; for example, enjoying our children and grandchildren, growing spiritually, continuing to contribute in some way until we die, staying healthy longer to enjoy ourselves without pain in our later years. All of these lifetime goals need attention at any age so that we can realize our dreams throughout our lives.

Our desires change with every chapter, and that's the time to change our direction or our chapter goals. Our needs change within our chapter as well. And, of course, our work life probably needs to change too.

We should always consider our desires as well as our needs. We aren't honest with ourselves if we don't confront the reality of what's going on in this chapter of our career or work life. Ask these "get ya goin'" questions:

- Am I in "static survival"?
- Am I stuck?
- Am I growing?
- What do I need to learn to continue to develop and grow?
- Do I still like what I am doing professionally?
- Am I feeling passionate about what I am doing?

Hopefully these questions will encourage you to slow down and take a look at where you are now. Then do something to move ahead.

Slowing down does not mean that you should take a long time to process where you are and decide where you want to go next. Take time to look at yourself in the light of honesty and truth. Hold yourself in a "neutral mind" for a while. Let your brain take a rest, and allow your heart to figure out your genuine desires and needs. Take time to realize all the elements of your life that are within your control. Are the sails of your boat leveraging the wind to take you to the desired destination? Plan ahead as far as you can see while being "planted" on a secure foundation: your values and what you stand for. Be anchored in your values and aware of your life's purpose.

Creating a Purpose Plan for Life and Career

Start by asking these reflective questions. Write down your responses in your notebook. You can be as brief or detailed as you feel necessary, but write the responses down.

- What do you want to change?
- What do you want to grow?
- What things are wrong in your life that you want to correct?
- What are your unfulfilled dreams?
- What fun are you missing that you want to find again?
- What do you need in order to repair relationships?
- With whom do you need to share your love?

Now let me ask some questions about other areas of your personal and professional life.

- What is missing at work that you really want?
- What do you want to achieve in the next three to five years?
- What is getting in your way of achieving what you want?
- What do you need to change in order to move ahead?
- What strengths do you have that you can use in your work?
- What do you want to grow professionally?
- What technological knowledge do you need to get ahead?
- Is what you want good for you and your family?
- Will your desires fit with your personal planning?

The Planning Process

A short list of areas in your life to consider follows. Look through the list, ask yourself the tough questions, and choose ten to twelve areas that you want to do something about over the next three to five years, the next chapter of your life. Place a *D* next to the one that you definitely want to take action on, a *M* next to the "maybes," and a *N* next to the ones that don't resonate with you, you don't connect with, or you already have plenty of in your life. Here's the list. There is space at the end of the list so you can make up your own "purpose theme." Use a pencil and eraser. It's okay to change your mind.

	Having a great leisure life		Working with a team
	More freedom for myself		Putting my talents to work
	Participating in sports		Serving my community
	Financial independence		Receiving new training & learning
	Commitment to another person		Reaching professional goals
	Improving my natural environment		Becoming an entrepreneur
	Expressing my creativity		Expressing my visionary talent
	Caring about and for my siblings		Creating and doing my hobbies
	Having adventure in my life		Getting regular exercise
	Living an exciting life		Managing my stress
	Trusting in myself and others		Staying healthy
	Exploring & growing my spirituality		Becoming a whole person
	Caring for others		Developing my legacy
	Volunteering in a meaningful way		Make a difference in many ways
	Being more playful		Being alone, just for me
	Forgiving myself or others		Balancing personal & work life

	Having peace within me		Being a closer friend to my friends
	Getting it right with me & others		Creating a whole new life or work
	Expressing my sexuality		Growing a close family
	Participating more in church		Planning life after retirement
	Simplify my life or get organized		Owning a home or property
	Improving my self-esteem		Managing my power
	Rebuilding relationships		Empowering others
	Expressing myself in new ways		Developing the potential in others
	Laughing more		Building something that lasts

Make up your own.

Choose twenty-five areas initially but let them compete for your attention, and then narrow the list down to between ten and twelve. Your next task is to write down the themes in the format shown below. Then write down or draw the picture that you want to achieve for visualizing the outcome of your efforts. Build the action plans now. List two, three, or four actions you can take to explore or actualize the purpose theme. Identify the time period you will commit to for accomplishing each action. This action planning process is a simple way to move ahead on what is most important to you at this time. Take some reflective "alone time" to complete the purpose plan.

The top ten to twelve purpose themes focus on the important areas for this chapter of your life. The list should reveal your authenticity and what is meaningful in your life. Write down your purpose themes, as demonstrated below.

Purpose theme name	Visualization of the purpose outcomes	Action Steps	Timing
Financial Independence	Seeing myself on a porch overlooking the ocean, talking to my spouse about doing anything you want to do.	Locate a financial advisor who is objective and not an insurance or stock broker. Establish a Roth IRA Find out my current wealth whatever it may be.	Within 6 months
Career Satisfaction	I see myself surrounded by my team of great people on a platform above the tallest building in the city. You are all getting bigger and bigger together.	Meet with my boss to discuss growth opportunities. Take an assessment to evaluate my strengths and then create a development plan. Find a mentor to help me within the company.	Next week Next month Within 3 months

Parenting with love and understanding	I see myself as an elder, with my children and grandchildren around me. They are all thanking me for being a good and loving parent.	Talk with each of the 3 kids alone for 2 hours a week.	Now
		Read 3 books on parenting.	Within 12 months
		Plan something special or a surprise that is fun and adventurous for the whole family every year.	By May
And so on			

This thoughtful process explores what is currently happening in your life and work. This is an opportunity to make those things right in your life. It's time to take charge and make things happen. Planning this next life chapter will be a journey of discovery, as well as an action plan for the things you want or need that provides the foundation for making the right choices. Your purpose plan will provide the anchor for managing the changes that will come along over the next few years or so. Write your script for living, and act out the script. If you don't have a plan, you just wander through life. It's not much different from what happens at work. You must plan the work or else a great deal of resources could be wasted. Don't waste time in your life. Take the actions to actualize the important priorities that you want.

The world is changing faster and faster, and you need realize that you will be impacted by the forces around you more frequently than in the past. Most of the younger generation will have seven to ten different careers and employers throughout their lifetime. It just doesn't pay to plan too far ahead, except in the areas of financial and family responsibilities. Even the way you take care of your family will change over time. The speed of changes in your life is increasing as you move ahead. A chapter in your life may last six months or six years. It will depend on the work you do and the lifestyle you choose for your family. Look for the opportunity to control what you can control and stay flexible about the things you can't control. Then set sail and execute your plan by making choices that take you in the direction you want to go. Plan your life in chapters rather than for the rest of your life.

You can't see what's in store for your whole life. That's why you should plan ahead as far as you can see. If you don't change the chapter, someone or some event(s) will change it for you, such as the global financial crises, 9/08 and 2011. Control what is important as far into the future as practical.

The last segment of this purpose planning exercise is to develop a purpose statement that summarizes your action plan themes. When anyone asks you "What is your purpose?" you can quickly respond, "My purpose is ..."

Here's an example: "The purpose of my family for the next five years is to grow individually as well as a family; learning from each other, enriching our love for one another and sharing our abundance, no matter what it is." This is a capstone to the exercise. It will be aligned with the vision you created at the outset and hold your intention in order to support your activities.

Streamline Success: Integrate the Professional with the Personal

— *Integrating Your Professional Development*

Professional development planning needs to be integrated into personal life plans. You spend more waking hours at work than you do at home. Work is part of life, of course. You complicate your life if you try to completely separate it or don't realize that it's better to be the same person at work as you are at home. Create your personal plans first, and then integrate the professional plan. Professional plans will most likely involve professional development. Since you spend so much of your life at work, search for meaning and purpose in your work life.

Wendy and David Ulrich, in their book *The Why of Work, How Great Leaders Build Abundant Organizations That Win,* describe the value of finding meaning and purpose in the work we do. "Thus the search for meaning adds value in two senses of the word. First, humans are meaning-making machines who find *inherent value* in making sense out of life. The meaning we make of an experience determines its impact on us and can turn disaster into opportunity, loss into hope, failure into learning, boredom into reflection. The meaning we create can make life feel rich and full regardless of our external circumstances or give us the courage to change out external circumstances. When we find meaning in our work, we find meaning in life."[25]

— *Aligning Values*

As I mentioned previously, values are the stabilizing factors during transitions. Our values need to be connected with the values of the business in which we work in order for us to be productive and maintain a great attitude about our work.

Here's an example of misaligned values. A woman joined a nonprofit organization as a member of the leadership team. She thought that the values espoused by the organization were aligned with hers. The way the CEO treated women leaders as compared to the men conflicted with those values. The CEO typically favored the men, even though his words seemed to be the right words. The women on the leadership team exceeded revenue and profit goals and surpassed their male counterparts. The men were compensated more than the women. Also, the leaders knew his wife very well. He seemed like a good family man until a convention or conference was on the schedule. Then he openly brought his "conference wife" with him. These uncomfortable situations inhibited the woman's productivity and creativity. She was always guarded and very cautious. Her CEO had a big integrity issue that she rejected, and she quit her job because of those conflicting values.

We try to align with the company values as closely as we possibly can so we can be energized about our work and the people with whom we work. Just as a company needs to align the annual strategies to everyone's performance goals and objectives, individual values need to be aligned in order to operate at our highest levels and be the best that we can be. Progressive CEOs recognize the importance of aligning company values

25 Ulrich, David and Wendy, *The Why of Work, How Great Leaders Build Abundant Organizations That Win*, McGraw Hill, 2010.

with personal values and insist that behavior matches those values. They also want recruiters and managers to hire people who have similar values as the company.

CEOs know that these factors improve the bottom line, as well as create a productive working environment. Some CEOs want the company's purpose to fulfill the employee's purpose in the work they do. Passionate workers take the initiative to do the right things for the business. Passionate people don't need to be managed closely, just given direction. That is a leader's dream!

David and Wendy Ulrich reinforce this concept in their book. "In addition to inherent value, meaning has *market value.* Meaningful work solves real problems, contributes real benefits, and thus adds real value to customers and investors. Employees who find meaning in their work are more satisfied, more engaged, and in turn more productive. They work harder, smarter, more passionately and creatively. They learn and adapt. They are more connected to customer needs. And they stick around. Leaders invest in meaning making not only because it is noble but also because it is profitable. Making sense can also make cents."[26]

– *Size and Fit*

You may be in a quandary about whether you should work for a large corporation, a medium-size company, a small business, or as an entrepreneur. Compare other options to the environment that you are in now. If you are considering switching to another size company, you need to look at several characteristics of each type of company. Basically, you are looking for a better fit for this chapter of your life or for the future chapter you are currently designing. Start with yourself. Look at your past experiences and evaluate the results. Knowing yourself as well as you now do, seek a type of company that allows you to express your talent and fulfill your purpose for this chapter of your life. Large, medium, or small may not be the relevant choices. We tend to think that one size may be better than another. In reality, size won't make that much difference; you may find the right environment for you in any size company. Some large corporations

---

26   Ulrich, *The why of Work, How Great Leaders Build Abundant Organizations That Win.*

can offer a great entrepreneurial orientation and business model. Some medium-size companies are very traditional and conservative.

Here are a few simple questions to ask when you are trying to find the right environment for you.

- Does this business align with my values, talents, and purpose?

- What are the genuine purpose, vision, and long-term growth path for this business?

- Is the top leadership of the business passionate, cohesive and aligned in their perceptions of how the business should operate? Do their business model and plans deal in reality?

- Does my future boss reflect the values expressed by senior management in a consistent manor?

- How much room will I have to grow in the business using my talents and energy?

- Will management allow me to have sufficient control over the work I do in order to express myself and my purpose within the boundaries of the work to be done?

It takes persistence to discover the answers to most of these questions. The answers may not have anything to do with the size of the company. You need to investigate companies in great depth. Be careful not to place halos around a company you think you'd love to work for. Remain stubbornly objective. Also, make very sure you are representing the real you to the company. They may decide that you are not a good fit for their environment or their purposes. This is a good decision, not a rejection. Respect the fact that the company helped you make the right choice by not giving you an offer.

Tolerance for Risk

Your tolerance for risk is something only you can determine. It's an important factor in deciding the environment in which you will thrive at work. There are not necessarily more risks in a smaller company. Large corporations are merging or getting gobbled up by other large companies every month. The plan is to find an environment in which you can thrive and succeed. Another chapter of your life will come along, and you'll make different choices at that time.

Objective Perspective

You should get feedback from others you know or work with. In a professional setting, 360-degree feedback instrument methods are common. I find that a coach can collect more relevant information than an online 360-degree assessment. I interview five to ten people at a variety of levels whom my clients suggest I speak to in order to learn more about them. My clients find that straight talk feedback is more valuable than any other they receive. You can do the same thing by having someone else ask colleagues to provide feedback about you.

Leave yourself vulnerable during your assessment process. Don't become defensive. Listen to the data, facts, and feedback and identify recurring information to determine trends and connections. Look for examples of where you have excelled. Seek occasions where you have had great satisfaction in something you did or helped others do. Let all of the information and your past experiences funnel down to five or six of your key talents. These are your gifts.

View of Your Current Situation

Your current boss may be a great source of information and feedback. You could be in the right job now but don't realize it. Surprise! Your perspective about your work may be the problem. Maybe you haven't developed the right attitude toward the purpose of your work. I have had clients be able to refresh themselves in their current roles and enhance their contributions to the business. Many have eventually been promoted. There goes the Peter Principle out the window again. Bosses can be your biggest supporters in your growth, so give them a chance. You may be inhibiting the important dialogue that needs to happen. Bosses can help and listen if you slow them down in order to have a meaningful conversation. Don't wait until your next performance review. Have periodic conversations about your development throughout the year. Try it. It works for many people.

Not all bosses will be helpful to you, but give them a chance. Correlate their feedback with that from others you trust and respect. If the boss can't help, and if the environment isn't right for you to excel, then you probably need to find another opportunity if there are no other positions available in the company. Your goals for this chapter of life will also guide your decision to leave your current job.

Don't look back once you have made your choice, whether you stay or make a change to another company. At times you may have some remorse about your choice. This is a common feeling after making a major decision. The feeling goes away when you start taking actions that move you to where you want to go. The past was your teacher. Respect the past, but move on into your future. Don't feel guilty about leaving the past behind. There should be no guilt in your life. Guilt is a wasted emotion if you are doing the right thing for yourself and you family.

Make Room for Your Family

Just as your purpose is important to moving ahead, the family has a purpose as well. Let's spend time on purpose planning for the family. How do you do this? There are probably many ways of approaching this reflective exercise. I suggest you start with a vision of what you want your family to be doing in five years. You may look further out than this, but I suggest you start with a five-year vision first. It will be easier to get your thoughts around a five-year time frame. If you like, use a two- or three-year time frame. Develop a detailed picture of what you see going on within your family in your chosen time frame. Write down specific activities that are going on. What do you see your family members doing? Have fun with the exercise; dream your dreams. Draw or cut out pictures from magazines to literally create a picture of the future. Consider doing the exercise with your spouse. Develop your plan as a loving team and partnership. Keep the picture handy. You need to be reminded of dreams that point to your purpose.

Work backwards, figuring out what needs to be accomplished or identify actions to fulfill the picture. Each year will be filled with activities, preparations, and purposes for that year. Go on to year two to think through what needs to be happening each year to reach your time frame. You may be surprised when the end of the first year approaches and you notice that you are behind schedule. Don't get anxious; adjust the plan. Also, be cautious about overcommitting. Be realistic. Consider the all-important values you embrace that will be passed on to other family members as they grow. Be sure to integrate these values into the family purpose plan.

You may encounter many things during this exercise that surprise you. You may realize that you never slowed down or took the time in the past to explore these opportunities. Maybe some obstacles were not apparent in the past. These discoveries help adjust your plans as you move toward the possibilities and removing the barriers.

Make Room for Flexibility

There is a strong need in this fast-changing world for continuous learning. This promotes growth in skills as well as experience, attitudes, and thinking. You need to develop different ways of thinking about work because many external forces will change the way you do business. Customer needs change, as do the needs of the workforce. For this reason you can't be stuck in the past; you need to renew yourself to learn and think differently. Continue to embrace your values and the authentic person you really are. This should not change much over the period of a chapter in your life. The business world requires leaders and managers to be flexible to the external world of change and competition. Leaders must also have the capacity to listen to the needs of the people who work for them. Being flexible and changing your thinking to look *forward* is important at work. Be aware of the "emergent" workforce, just as you need to be aware of your children growing up with digital accessories and global economics.

Spherion and Harris Interactive[27] started to study the changing workforce in 1997 and called the new workforce "emergent" mentality. There are emergent employees and emergent employers, in contrast to traditional employees and employers. Without getting into too much detail, emergent workers are emphasizing work/life balance, demanding

---

27   Spherion and Harris Interactive study, 1997, Chapter 6, page 11.

more support for their work and personal lives, want flexibility and career growth development and to be rewarded for their contributions. The emergent workers are found at any age and gender. Motivations are changing. If you aren't listening and are not flexible to the changing environment, you may be at risk of not adjusting to the changes.

The point of this is that it's necessary to be flexible and willing to change in order to plan your life and the way you work. You must be engaged in professional development. Continuous learning is a must, not an option. You can't depend on what you learned even three years ago. Keep up with your children, as well as the external forces in this "information/digital age" that compound our need for continuous learning.

The global populations over thirty-five are "immigrants" to the digital culture. They may learn and use bits and pieces, but they do not think in digital terms. The digital "natives" are harnessed comfortably with PCs, MP3 players, iPhones, iPods, downloads, uploads, instant messaging, text messaging, and a digital language of their own. If we don't pay attention to this trend and understand the impact on our family life and the global society, we will become stagnant and easily replaced with a more progressive-thinking person.

Business models must also contain the flexibility to change. You can develop an organizational plan similar to your personal purpose plan. The elements are similar. There is a cycle for a business that is similar to a chapter in a life. Usually the planning for a chapter of a company can only project out three years or less. The fundamental values and vision of the organization may be embraced long-term, but the way the business operates or is managed may need more frequent adjustments in order to stay competitive and meet the reality of a changing and emergent workforce. The purpose of a business is the vision. The mission is more long-term. Shorter-term strategies are usually annual, but I can see strategies being reevaluated and changed mid-year in certain companies that need to be technically advanced.

- Plan ahead no further than you can reasonably see.

- Don't overcommit: have reasonable objectives.

- Choose the right tools for the work to be done.

Consider both technical and nontechnical tools

Spend more time thinking about what tools you really need to do your work. Not every advanced process or system is electronic. There are many tools that help you design and execute your work without being computerized. Look into many avenues, not just technical choices. As an example, all the thoughtful processes we've discussed here are systems to help you be more productive without being digitized.

What's the purpose?

Some of these devices are just toys for your amusement. Toys can be fun, if that's your intention. As you know, technology toys can be expensive. Toys can cost more than just the price tag. Ask yourself: Is this device taking me toward my objectives? Will this take time away from my family because I intend to enjoy more family time? Will this pull me in the wrong direction? Remember, your plan is to stay on track with what you want to accomplish. Make the right choice depending on whether the technology will enrich you, your family, or your work.

The technological tools you use can absolutely help you to be more productive and stay in control. Multitasking devices are common reasons for choosing a personal electronic device. It may be useful if multitasking is inherent in the device. Let the device multitask, not you. We discussed the impact of multitasking in a previous chapter. It's my opinion that humans are not made to perform multitasking as a way of living and working. Be cautious. You may be falling into a trap that may lead you toward unimportant activities and busyness.

Technology is supposed to be the slave of the modern age. But this "techno slave" needs to be fed, maintained, and cared for. That takes time. Aligning your choice of "techno slaves" with your mission is the first step in the decision-making process. Does this fit in with where you need to go? Just because someone else said that this technology is the latest and greatest is not the reason to accept it. Proving the technology works is not as important as the need for and productive uses of the devices. Try to truly understand that this technology is the means to the end. The desired outcomes must come into play when struggling with the choices. What will life or work become with the device or without the device? Will this enhance or detract for your purpose plan?

Electronic and mechanical devices are of course necessary and extremely helpful in communicating and processing the work that must get done. Test new devices before jumping in and buying or accepting one from your employer. Try it out before you use it. Ask others about the advantages and disadvantages of the tool. Ask them how the device has made them more effective, as well as about the frustration, stress, and investment of time needed to learn how to use it. Again, ask tough questions of others, as well as yourself. People who are already using the device will usually support it because they made the investment. Just make sure you buy a device or software that will help you operate more effectively without adding more headaches to your days.

My Story

I am a sucker for salespeople offering new ways to save time and make me more productive. Maybe I'm gullible because I was a sales representative for seven years of my professional life. My wife is very practical and appropriately questions me about what I may be excited to purchase. She asks tough questions, such as:

- What will this do for you?

- What will this *really* do for you? Do you need it now?

- How much does this cost?

- When can you expect a return on you investment in terms of purchasing it and the time needed to learn how to use it?

- Will you need to pay someone to teach you how to use it? Is it speed that you want, or is it efficiency you need to improve?

- Is this technology in your business plan or budget for the year?

- Have you budgeted enough for the investment?

I'm exhausted! But slowing down to answer her questions is the right thing to do and ends up having great value.

I may make an emotional purchase because it is cool to own or use it. Yes, I have an iPhone, laptop, desktop printers, and the software to do my work. But I don't have useless software anymore, although I did in the past. I now ask users for their opinions and their uses, as they may be different from mine. The point is that I have learned to slow down and think about the actual need for the technical tools I *think* I may need. I stopped making impulsive purchases.

- Test them.
- Ask others about their experiences.
- Don't make an "emotional purchase."

Make Sure the Time is Right

Timing for acquiring the device is also important to consider. Your organization may not be ready for it. The technology may force changes in the organization that will be difficult to implement, costly in the way of poor morale, and stressful when it impacts the values and culture of the company. Companies and individuals rarely slow down enough to consider these important factors. Don't let technology just "happen" to you. Make good choices. I've learned in my corporate career not to introduce a new concept, program, or process unless the organization is ready to accept it as being helpful.

Time to Pause

Review, complete, and adjust your written plan for the next chapter of your life.

Plan your technical and organization needs.

Part IV
Maintaining Purpose and Progress

9
Stick To Your Plan

Planning and executing your plan is living life. You move ahead based on your values, priorities, and purpose. Focus on what is right for you and your family.

Staying the course while executing your plan takes discipline.

"Vision without execution is hallucination" – Thomas A. Edison

You have a vision: action steps and timetables to focus your energy. As you move forward and start accomplishing your goals, you gain encouragement that creates momentum. You start to see changes in your life and work that release energy and passion. This is where you want to be. From time to time you may need to refresh your plans and actions. This is progress. Celebrate the milestones as you progress. Celebrate the small steps as well as the big achievements. Continuously reach for more when you are satisfied with your progress, growth, contributions, and feelings of worth.

Visualize Success

It is very helpful to actually visualize what you want in your future. Creating pictures of what you want in life provides a constant reminder of where you want to go. Have fun—draw a picture or cut out pictures:

imbed these pictures in your thoughts and heart. Your subconscious mind will take over and start making things happen to fulfill the promise of the picture. The way it works is sometimes called "magical."

Norman Vincent Peale, in his 1982 book *How to Make Positive Imaging Work for You,*[28] wrote, "Imaging, the forming of mental pictures or images, is based on the principle that there is a deep tendency in human nature to ultimately become precisely like that which we imagine ourselves as being. An image formed and held tenaciously in the conscious mind will pass presently, by a process of mental osmosis, into the unconscious mind. And when it is accepted firmly in the unconscious, the individual will strongly tend to heave it, for then it has you." He goes on to emphasize this power. "Imaging is positive thinking carried on step further. In imaging, one does not merely think about a hoped-for goal; one 'sees' or visualizes it with tremendous intensity, reinforced by prayer. Imaging is a kind of laser beam of the imagination, a shaft of mental energy in which the desired goal or outcome is pictured so vividly by the conscious mind that the unconscious mind accepts it and is activated by it. This releases powerful internal forces that can bring about astonishing changes in the life of the person who is doing the imaging."

Visualize Using Your Gifts

Slow down to visualize the outcomes of using your gifts to fulfill your desires for yourself, family, and work. Use the Law of Attraction to work for you. The law states that you can have what you want much easier if you have a clear picture of what you want and start placing yourself in that picture now. "The Law of Attraction delivers to you precisely what you ask it to. Change your thoughts and you will change your world. It is an extremely simple process. It is do-able and you can do it. Learn it, properly implement it, and you will prosper above and beyond what you previously 'believed' to be possible."[29]

"Live your dream" is another way of expressing it. Live the life you picture as if you have it now. Things come into your life more easily when

---

28 Peale, Norman Vincent, *How to Make Positive Imaging Work for You,* Originally published by Fleming H. Revell Company, 1982. Formerly published under the title, *Dynamic Imaging and Positive Imaging,* page 5.

29 "The Power of Thoughts," http://www.abundance-and-happiness.com.

you are positive about what you want. Focus more on what you do want rather than what you don't want in your life. Focusing your mind and emotions on the negative is a drag. Use positive energy to bring things into your life as you pursue your purpose. Pray for help. Thank God for what you have and what you will have.

"What do I really want?" is a great question to frequently and repeatedly ask yourself. The question slows you down, and your response refocuses you on what's important. You may overly complicate your life and work if you don't know what you really want.

What do you want to get out of this conversation?

What do you want to get out of this meeting?

Focusing on "what you really want" is helpful in simplifying the situation, clarifying your purpose, and finding common ground with others.

What do you want to get out of your purpose plan?

Prepare and Execute the Plan

Preparing for the journey also includes creating the good habits of execution. Visualizing the outcomes of your plans will help you start living them. Start living life as if you have already attained what you want in life. Activate all of your inner energy. This is why I want you to produce a visual for every purpose theme you choose. Put the subconscious to work. Allow things to come into your life, and be attentive to how they may help you. This is the law of attraction working for you. Wikipedia describes the law of attraction in this overview.

The Law of Attraction claims to have roots in quantum physics.[30] "According to proponents of this law, thoughts have an energy which attracts whatever it is the person is thinking of. In order to control this energy to one's advantage, proponents state that people must practice four things:

1. Know exactly what you want.

2. Ask the universe for it.

---

30 Quantum Physics,http://en.wikipedia.org/wiki/Law_of_Attraction-cite_note-9#cite_note-9.

3. Feel, behave, and know as if the object of your desire is already yours (visualize).

4. Be open to receive it and let go of (the attachment to) the outcome.

"Thinking of what one does not have, they say, manifests itself in not having, while if one abides by these principles, and avoids "negative" thoughts, the universe will manifest a person's desires."[31]

You've frequently heard these phrases in the sports world: "You need to believe." "We believe." This is a way of knowing that your plans will be realized. Use this energy. It creates the passion that takes you to where you want to go. Your passion is also contagious to others. They will bring things into your life and work through inspiration because you are living a life with purpose and intention, tenaciously executing your plan.

Try to visualize how you'd like the chapter of your life to develop and play out. These visuals, just like the sailboat for the Life Control Model, will develop while you prepare your purpose plans and actions. Visualizing the pictures you want in your life helps you center on what's important. It also helps you make the day-to-day choices that are right for you. Visualizing is a method of screening out wasted efforts and screening in opportunities that will accelerate progress.

The pictures you design are fundamental to the stories you will develop around what you want in life. Stories you tell yourself are the programs in your mind that focus on what is right for you and what is not. Be cautious about the stories created. Make sure they support your purpose and mission. Wrong or misguided stories inhibit moving in the desired direction. The pictures and stories provide channel markers for sailing in the right direction. Having plans, pictures, and stories indicating your direction provides structure that manifests itself as the outcomes you want. This is the reason I use the sailboat for the Life Control Model. It creates a picture that reminds us of many concepts and meanings: what you can and can not control.

---

31 http://en.wikipedia.org/wiki/Law_of_Attraction-cite_note-gazette2-10#cite_note-gazette2-10.

Picture the Goals

Let's look at how a leader can keep people in the company focused on the outcomes of the annual strategy or mission. First, it's important for you to know why you are doing certain work. Leaders must then help you stay focused; not only on why and where you are going but also on how you execute the work. Usually you are left on your own to do the work. Good leaders continuously remind others of the purpose and direction. It's your role as a leader to figure out how to fulfill the mission with the help of others through their cooperation and collaboration. Leaders must create and communicate *pictures* of the outcomes or goals of the organization. You may have seen pictures on the office walls that describe the strategy or goals. Some corporations have spent over one million dollars to print and post the pictures of the journey of the mission on the interior walls of the buildings. They want the mission understood in simple terms you can picture in your mind. It works.

Why shouldn't you do this for your personal life? Pictures of your future plans and desires help you navigate the journey. Integrating your personal and professional purposes is important to have appropriate balance and control of life. It's easy to let business or work life control your personal life. It's not difficult to lose perspective of what is right for you or even what may be right for the business. Fooling yourself into thinking that your work life is the most important because it facilitates survival can warp your perspective. It can also blow you off course from where you really want to go. You can become a workaholic, working yourself so hard that it impacts family life.

Have Confidence

Of course, a plan without action is wasted effort. Intellectually, we all know this. Taking action is "where the rubber meets the road." This is usually an uncomfortable time. You may be taking risks, making tough choices, and confronting barriers that are preventing you from moving ahead. You need confidence that you are doing the right things and courage to take actions that may not be popular with your friends, colleagues, or boss. You may move against the culture or have conflicts with distractions around you. Courage will help you endure the pace and provide you with the fortitude you'll need to succeed. This process can be an exciting journey if you make it so.

If you get derailed, getting back on track and knowing that you are in synch again with your plan will provide confidence. Confidence is energizing. It helps you remain passionate about what you are working toward. Confidence helps you choose the right priorities, based on your purpose as well as your values, and maintain your focus. Living life based on your values and priorities brings control. It's an open and honest way of living your life. "Show up" with confidence for what you really stand for every time you are tested by conflicting values, interruptions in your direction, and, at times, ethical dilemmas. You move forward with confidence when you are on the right path for you, your family, and your professional life.

Risks and Courage

You need to take some risks when you step out and move in new directions. You could be frightened of what you plan to do. So how do you get through it? One step at a time is a good way to negotiate the trepidation. Each time you forge ahead and take those risks, you start realizing that they aren't really big risks. The next challenge may also be daunting, but you have gained confidence that you can overcome the next barrier. Of course you may be afraid of launching into some exciting new direction in your personal life as well. The same feelings occur in your gut, but as you bust through every barrier the results will be worth the challenge.

We can come up against some barriers that we can't overcome. That is the time to slow down and take a close look at what is going on. We may not be taking the right action for the right reason. Reassessing our actions is more appropriate than calling the action a failure. The experience we may consider bad for us may really be an opportunity for us to learn more about ourselves and the value of our purpose plans. The speed of change may be catching up with our plans. We may need to accelerate our progress, make adjustments to the plans, or realize the actions are not worth the originally intended outcomes.

Taking risks is common when setting a new course of direction. Risk will always be there, so make friends with it. Be careful to not let risk overwhelm you. If you are dealing with reality, you can control the degree of risk. For example, slow down if you feel you are going too fast. Make adjustments to your execution plan.

Consider Long Term versus Short Term

We need to contrast short-term and long-term business planning to acknowledge the importance of each. Short-term thinking that generates short-term results may sacrifice long-term results. Of course, we need short-term results with many projects as part of a long-range goal or long-term project. Long-term goals need milestones, which are shorter-term objectives. What frequently happens is that the long-term purpose or mission becomes obscure. A leader's role is to get the short-term work done while keeping people focused on the long-term results. Our personal role is similar: producing step-by-step actions that take us closer to our personal goals or mission.

Decisions that impact short-term results are usually made quickly. If you need to add more resources to complete a project, you may say go ahead and add it, without considering the extra cost if it seems negligible. It won't make that much difference and the project must be completed on time. In a crisis, we all need to react fast. I'm talking, however, about an important choice to be considered for long-term goal achievement. As you look back on your experiences, most of the time the quick decisions may not have been the best choices for you, others, or a project.

Prioritize

After you decide to make the changes you have reflected on, you need to prioritize the actions. Make sure you are executing *fundamental* changes first. Focusing on your most important priorities will enable you to maintain the right direction. Focusing on the fundamental key activities will ensure that you reach your goals in a productive manner. Being busy with purposeful actions is very productive. Focusing on "what will make a difference" is a great way of looking at our actions and activities to maintain productivity. We won't waste time.

John Kotter's[32] first principle for large-scale change is to establish

---

32 Kotter, *Leading Change.*

urgency. We can apply this principle to executing our plans. Urgency is inherent in priorities; they are "must do's," not optional.

Creepers

Beware of "creepers." You may be familiar with the term "scope creep." Scope creep is when the project expands beyond the original mission or intension. Many exciting ideas come to the forefront in the course of executing a plan or project. Filtering new ideas and suggestions through a long-term mission "screen" gives you a method for slowing down in order to remain focused. When this happens, ask some questions about these "creepers."

- Do these ideas, initiatives, or actions enhance our short-term and long-term goals?

- Will these actions or proposals replace other project initiatives and in what way?

- Will this initiative fulfill our purpose, or will it distract our attention, energy, and resources?

Skunk works is a widely used term in business, engineering, and technical fields to describe a group of people within an organization that is given a high degree of autonomy, unhampered by bureaucracy, and tasked with working on a project that is hoped to be innovative and/or out of the ordinary. I know that skunk works have some advantages for innovating new or improved products, but be cautious of the resources and attention being diverted at the sacrifice of the on-time execution of the plan outcomes. Stay purpose focused. Peripheral opportunities should be considered but not at the risk of accomplishing the mission.

Business executives call me in to consult during the execution phase because they need help with maintaining focus on the strategies and long-term goals. They fear that they will get diverted by minor projects, like skunk works or creepers that increase the scope of the mission or waste valuable resources. I help them develop structure and focus that keep them on track with what they said they wanted to do.

Notice What Slows You Down

Throughout our cycle of personal and professional life we collect "barnacles." Barnacles are live crustaceans that cling to the hull of a boat and grow. Barnacles can take the form of bad habits, outdated skills, unusable stuff in the basement or garage, or sometimes friends that we really don't value anymore. We can also see the "cookies" we collect through the Internet or when we install new software. After awhile we need to clean off these accumulations from wherever they collect. They will eventually slow us down. The barnacles need to be scrubbed off of the boat's hull and the cookies deleted from our computer system. They are a drag on our systems and our progress. They are the creepers that steal our energy. This can happen to us all if we lose focus. We can get caught up in busyness or entertain ideas and initiatives that will eat up the energy we need to succeed in life as well as work

There are times when standing fast is the right thing to do. Screening out creepers is a concept that brings an awareness to help you be discerning about choices, including whether to add something or make a slight change in direction because the situation or environment has changed or brought you a great opportunity to consider. Flexibility is needed here. If it fulfills your purpose or enhances the desired outcome, then a new initiative may be the right choice. Slow down to consider it. Making a shift in your direction may be the right thing to do. The direction adjustment may improve your original plan.

Collaboration

Slow down to understand the stakeholders. We all receive information and listen a little differently because of our backgrounds and experiences. Be sensitive to what people may need to effectively collaborate, understand, and move ahead. It's a good idea to simply ask the stakeholders how they would like you to stay in contact or communicate. Then it's up to you to adjust your approach for certain people. Maintain an open dialogue as you execute a project. Listening is also part of communicating, as well as explaining, so listen. Also, invest time in keeping others informed about your activities and progress.

Around every technology and work process there are people who are engaged in productive work. Be aware of the consequences of what you produce and how you produce it. This is where communication is critical to the success of your projects, as well as personal success. Collaborating with others for a variety of reasons engages them in a way that makes them feel a part of what you are trying to accomplish. Show that you care about them and indicate how they can impact the projects or tasks. Communication needs to include a continuous dialogue about what is happening. Take time to answer questions for clear understanding.

Collaborating and Technology

Remember to use technology to communicate in the way your audience wants you to. This may not be the way you want to communicate with others. In many businesses today, the younger generations prefer to communicate by texting rather than using e-mail or even the phone. Older generations continue to prefer e-mail. I recently discovered that project teams, that need to frequently share information, are using Twitter groups to communicate. The message here is to be in tune with how your audience wants to receive the information you send them.

Use technology to enhance the project communication process by sending messages, asking questions and providing progress updates. Listening shows respect for others. Using the right technology to collaborate will demonstrate your sensitivity to how other people listen and connect with what you want to say.

It is also an opportunity to learn something that you may not have previously considered. Slowing down and using the appropriate technology to listen and explain demonstrates that you care about the individuals involved in the work. You wouldn't launch a new widget into the market place without market testing. When you test the market you listen to customers and design the marketing and sales campaigns around responses to the product or service. You are sensitive to the needs of the customer. You may even adjust the product to make it more accepted by the customers. Why shouldn't you do similar testing within your own company to see how the users will like the end product, policy, or outcome? Consider the feedback and make appropriate adjustments to the product or service.

Work Smart

Listening closely to the people working among us is vital to being productive. Management frequently doesn't sufficiently listen to the people doing the work. They may ignore the wisdom of the worker that they have hired to "work smart" and "perform with excellence." It may be time for the person actually doing the work to step up and ask the uncomfortable questions. You need to seek the truth and deliver the truth to your boss. Just saying "okay" to the boss's request isn't the answer to the problem. If you feel responsible for helping the business and the customer, you need to ask questions and provide your opinion. Managers need to listen to people performing the work and integrate what they learn with the changes that top management is requiring. You will be uncomfortable, but as you've learned, that's the right thing to do. Focus on the long-term objectives and remind others of the purpose or mission. You need to slow down, even if it is contrary to management's view. "Work smart." Isn't that what our boss and leaders want us to do?

Working smart will always involve focusing on priorities instead of superficial activities. We all need to focus on our priorities first. And we really can't have twenty top priorities. That's shotgunning the mission. Confronting the reality and describing impact and consequences will resolve questions about what's most important to work on. I suggest my clients focus on the toughest or most important priorities that confront them each day. Some of the less important tasks may not get done that day or may never get done, and that's okay.

Say Something

Consider subtracting activities. You need to clearly make a choice of what you will not do. Your choice to stop doing something may place you in uncomfortable situations. You may frequently feel you are trapped in the middle and can't win. It is appropriate to think of these situations as healthy conflicts. Confront reality. If others aren't seeing reality, you are obligated, for the sake of the business, to ask the uncomfortable questions. Help others let go of the unproductive activities that should be screened out.

If your actions are not consistent with the culture or your manager's expectations, something is out of synch and needs to be addressed. Have a conversation with your manager to let her know what you are doing and why. Experiment with doing the work a different way to improve your productivity and share what you've learned with your manager and coworkers. This action can be considered healthy experimental pushback. It is useful in improving how tasks are accomplished to meet the desired outcomes.

Collaboration must happen in order to get clear understanding and iron out conflicts, so everyone can move ahead in the right direction for the right reasons. Make sure that everyone involved is working toward the same mission, goals, and objectives. Dialogue and collaboration generate better thinking and decision making.

Avoid Distractions

– *Technology*

Technology offers many tools that can be beneficial toward fulfilling your mission and day-to-day work. At the same time, technology can be a distraction. Discard technology that doesn't fit. Be cautious about using technology just because it's "cool" or you feel you must have it. Don't waste time on new technology that isn't meaningful to you or your work. In many cases we didn't need technical devices until we acquired them. Only then did they become necessary.

– *Internet Traps*

The Internet has changed the way business is done around the world and will continue to be the main highway of commerce and communications. It can also be a time trap if you get caught up in surfing, searching or reading things that may not make a difference in your work or life. Questions should pop up as you look at how you are using or misusing the Internet. There may be many reasons for workers being less productive besides the Internet, but the misuse of this tool is a common cause of productivity loss. Many large companies are trying desperately to control or curb this time waster. I remember speaking with an executive of a medium-size manufacturing business. He recently felt compelled to implement an Internet monitoring device on all employee computers after many of the office personnel had been laid off. He estimated that most office employees would gain one hour each day in productive work.

The Internet trap is in force when you are making useless connections with others and information sites or when you use it for entertainment at the wrong time. Internet sites can, of course, be used for entertainment or recreation when the time is right to do so.

Getting lost in cyberspace can happen to anyone. Some people may be addicted to it. Time flies by! Wandering around without purpose steals time away from focusing on your priorities. Spend your time advancing your objectives and moving in your intended direction. I don't mean that having fun doesn't have value. Fun is something everyone wants in life. If fun is in cyberspace, go for it at the right times, but have a good reason for surfing the Internet.

The right time to use the Internet or other electronic devices is "on demand." Situations require you to use this technology to fulfill the task. Searching the Internet can help you locate experts in the subject you are investigating. A focus will help you determine how to use the technology and speed the work you do in a thoughtful and productive way. Physicians, attorney, engineers, and other professionals will use the Internet through informatics more and more often as the systems become available. Wikipedia describes informatics in the medical field as, "Health informatics or medical informatics is the intersection of information science, computer science, and health care."

A cardiovascular surgeon I know is helping organizations develop informatics systems to help physicians. He said that "docs" can't know all they need to know, even though they are diagnosing patients every day. New medical technologies and treatments are being introduced in such high volume that physicians can't learn fast enough. Informatics will immediately bring the latest information to the physician and surgeons at the point they need it. They can then use their best judgment for diagnosing or determining a solution based on the most current data and clinical information. This is a wonderful use of technology.

— *Control Choice*

Devices can become vices. Controlling the impulse or rationalization you experience is key to making good choices throughout your day. Who's in control? Are you in control or is the technology in control? You must do the thinking even though artificial intelligence is imbedded in the software you're using. You think you are in command of the technology, but you can be sucked into becoming a slave of your devices. Focus on your mission and moving toward fulfilling your purpose. This focus helps you be discerning while staying in control.

Keep in mind that the devices may not be serving you as originally designed. At this point you need to take action and find replacements, substitutions, or updates for the device. Or decide to give up the device or software. Move on!

My Story

I worked with one of the most effective and well-known computer network experts in the United States. He didn't have a personal computer in his office. That seemed strange to me, so I asked why he didn't use one. He said that his role was to keep people developing and implementing the necessary changes and executing projects. He needed to think on a global scale most of the time. Projects were being implemented for worldwide operations. He needed to connect the right people and move them to work together effectively to fulfill the purpose of one of the largest networks in the world. The computer would distract him from his purpose.

You can also be distracted if you are not intentional about your actions and choices and the use of your time. The value of time is in how you use it. Don't focus on how time is wasted. Focus on how you can best use your time to complete your task, mission, and objective in order to lead a more productive and satisfying life. You can lose valuable time because some technology is dependent on you. I've spent too much time away from my family in the evening inputting information into a system that requires my attention. I tell myself, "I must get this done!" Well, most of the time there is a better time to input the data. The technology was starting to control me.

Reevaluate and Refocus

Slowing down periodically, or checking in with yourself, allows you to take a look at what you are doing. Then you can make better choices as to how you want to use your time. While navigating toward your mission, staying on course may have its frustrations. For example, feeling frustrated with interruptions is part of life. You just need to make the right choices when these interruptions seem to get in the way.

We can plan a car trip to destinations far away. We can't plan on the weather cooperating, but we bring an umbrella or rain gear along. We can set out on a sailing voyage; the wind may not cooperate, but that's why we carry a motor. We can prepare, but we can't control all of the events and situations. The long-term plan and a clear knowledge of the destination will keep us navigating in the right direction.

Time to Pause

What events frequently reoccur that distract you from pursuing your mission, purpose, or priorities?

What will you do to stop or control the distractions?

Review the technical devices you are currently using. Are the devices serving you in completing your mission?

What technology or maintenance is hindering your work?

Name three actions you can take to get more control over the devices and your time.

When will you change how you operate? Get moving!

10
Reassess Your Plan

In this fast-changing world, you must renew your plans, relationships, and skills to take you to the next level of your life and career. Look at relationships you value, your commitments, and what you want and need in your life. Revisit these areas frequently. This world keeps changing at a faster rate, and it's necessary to make more frequent adjustments in your life to maintain control while pursuing a satisfying life.

Face Change

Change happens. Barriers to our growth and development are always there. We can't give up when we encounter barriers but must make a choice to go around the barriers, confront and remove them, or blast them apart with drama. Whatever we face, opportunities to learn, grow, and become stronger will always remain.

Slow down to reflect, think, and test your plan. There needs to be some testing or discovery about what it will take to fulfill your plan. Renewal isn't just deciding what you will do and jumping into action. Explore the training, education, or experience needed to move into the next chapter of life. Reinforcing your plan with known resources will accelerate growth. You may find that your plan needs adjusting early on. It's great if you discover it early. At first you may feel stuck or that you're making a false start. There may be good reasons for some of this feeling. Listen to the feelings. They may let you know that the risks are too high or you may need to secure more resources before executing your plan.

When conditions change I suggest slowing down to revisit your purpose; then decide to act in a controlled and thoughtful manner. You will make the best choices when you consider the long-term impact of your actions. Finding mentors or those who have gone before you will help prepare your journey.

If you are having some internal conflict, you need to go deeper to figure out what is going on. It may not be a bad conflict; it may be a conflict that needs to be addressed immediately. Your conflict may also be with the place you are in the chapter of your life or work. Maybe it's time for a repurposing and moving into a new chapter. Ask yourself those tough questions again. Confront the conflicts. It may be time for a major change. Listen to the voice of your values. Think about what you see and what you don't see.

First, address reality with a few questions.

- What has changed?

- What has come into the situation that is unexpected?

- What is in my control and what is out of my control?

- What may be the consequences of making a change?

Also, seek someone to discuss your situation and what you may be struggling with. That is always helpful for thoughtful processing and making good choices.

Listen to Intrusions

When interruptions or intrusions creep in, listen for opportunities, because there may be a conflict in your plans that you may not yet be conscious of. These intrusions happen for a reason. Slow down and be aware. Listen to what is happening. These interruptions are going to happen throughout your journey. They may be short blips, just an irritant, or some clue that will become clearer in the future. Listen, reflect, and then decide whether some changes may need to occur. Then act. Plot a course that seems right for you at this time. Make the adjustments and move on it. Slow down periodically to make sure the course is correct, and keep moving forward; don't regret where you've been in the past. Learn from the past, but don't regret the past.

Be careful that you are not rationalizing your actions when you seem to be stuck. That can be an honest occurrence, but it can also be a danger to you. Rationalizing can mean you're lying to yourself or that you've figured it out after arguing with yourself and are now convinced that this direction is the right way to go. As mentioned before, your brain may lie to you. The only way you can move to the truth is to be completely honest with yourself. Slow down, get with someone you trust, and process the angst and arguments that may be going through your mind or subconscious.

Remove the Barriers

When you honestly hit a barrier that is more than a mere interruption, you need to remove the barrier in your path. This will take some energy and work. Don't put it off! Find some help, even pray about the obstacle. Locate someone, maybe a coach, to help you process and make choices. Maybe it's time to change your environment; get outside if you can and take a walk, or find a quiet place to think about your barriers. This may not be a one-time process. It may take multiple passes to find answers to your questions. Be persistent. There may be something in your past that you haven't gotten over or worked through yet. This processing may take more than a coach to help you. You may need psychotherapy with a professional. Recognize the barrier for what it is. Get to the core of the issue. Confronting the issue quickly and honestly removes the barriers and prevents you from sailing off course. Clean the barnacles from the bottom of your boat. Do something to set you free. Move on.

The Global Economy

The impact of the global economy has been with us for many years now. This expansive economy affects everyone in the United States, from the smallest rural communities to large metropolitan areas. It has changed the way you live. A global economy is something that stimulates fast, ongoing changes and frequent adjustments to how we live and work. Consequences of a global business environment have been low prices (since many products are made in low wage countries), job losses, companies merging in order to compete, foreign investment taking control of parts of your life, and on and on. The most notable consequence of a global economy was the September 2008 investment banking and Wall Street meltdown created by the subprime mortgage lending crisis. Personal lives around the world, as well as global financial structures, were affected. Within twelve hours, the United Kingdom, Russia, Japan, Mexico, and Canada were negatively impacted. Unfortunately, suicides occurred; people not only lost their homes but also saw their retirement savings dramatically erode. People around the world were scared about the potential of a worldwide depression. These uncontrollable events changed many lives forever.

This ongoing condition forces us to live differently, learn new skills, and shift our energy into new areas. We have become interdependent with many other countries. Technology is spurring changes in a dramatic way. Technological advances and the Internet have helped propel the United States into a global economy.

Communication capabilities are providing information to masses of potential readers almost instantly. Creativity in approaches to the marketplace is forcing traditional companies to be evaluative and reconsider what their business is all about. Companies are rethinking their purposes, as well as how to compete and improve operations. Competing is more complex because the players are around the world. Until 9/08, financial resources for business people with strong business plans seemed plentiful. Now businesses must observe, listen, and change plans, even their business model, in order to survive and thrive in this global environment. As a business leader, you must stay connected with global news, which affects your ability to change and your ability to innovate faster by managing the workforce in new ways.

Businesses in Crisis

The 9/08 financial crisis brought thousands of CEOs of small businesses, who were owners or major investors, to their knees. They were very worried about employees and their families. CEOs and small business owners assumed enormous pressures and responsibilities for human care and managing fear. They were not necessarily taking care of themselves very well either. Emotions were impacting families. Their worries and emotions were transferred to their employees, which made matters worse. They were out of control, sliding into hopelessness. This financial impact was repeated in July 2011.

CEOs from thousands of companies needed to get unstuck by taking creative, "out of the box" approaches to rethinking their business and its *purpose*. They were not going to sustain viable companies by doing what they'd done in the past, before the economic downturns and recession.

I lost business because of 9/08. It was necessary for me to change my intended strategy for 2009. I was forced to seek opportunities in the face of the changes in the global economy. I needed to pay the mortgage and eat. My strategy was to help businesses take advantage of the current conditions and to do business differently than they had done in the past. I also changed my lifestyle, as did many millions of other people, but my basic purpose plan didn't change. I changed my cycle of change within my larger cycle of change and my plans for continued growth. The tactical changes I made sustained my business. In 2010 I experienced a 30 percent growth over 2009. I have adjusted my approach to clients and the business community again in 2011 with continued success.

Families in Crisis

Most individuals who lost their jobs after 9/08 were rethinking their purpose and strengths and reassessing a variety of opportunities while feeling anxiety and fear. The process of recovery or renewal for business leaders parallels that of individuals. Both need to face reality, reassess their potential, make choices, take risks, build a new plan, and take action with as much energy as they can muster.

You can also look for the opportunities that globalization brings, as many have. Again, you have choices. Search for opportunities in the midst of the changes occurring around you.

Make some choices to adjust your plans. Your choices may launch you into a new chapter or change the direction of your business. When a manufacturing plant is closed because the work will be performed in another country, the impact on people is dramatic. The international financial crisis created tremendous job losses as well. When these decisions throw you into the street, there seem to be few choices. Recognizing the early signs of a business closing and preparing for it is still in your control. Before the plant closes, you must take actions that lead you to another opportunity. Step back and look at reality, adjust your plan, and take action.

The global economy helped me get a global client. On a visit to Singapore, I gave a workshop for a multinational company. That company later became a client for a short time. It really didn't matter to them that I did not live in Singapore. Technology allowed me to perform most of the work from my office. I maneuvered the global network to fit into my network; the network didn't force me to adapt. My business model may change again. I will also be looking for more of those surprise opportunities. I'd like you to seek similar opportunities by being aware of the changes occurring around you and taking advantage of changing market conditions.

Leading and Communicating Change
— *Facing Change in Business*

At times during your career you will question what you are doing and the direction you are heading. You become disillusioned or out of synch. Sometimes you whine about how you are feeling. That is the time to face what is going on, because change is in your future. If you don't take these feeling seriously and take some action, you may be miserable at work for a long time. Get refreshed. You may not be growing. This work may not be fulfilling your current or newly discovered passion.

If your passion doesn't fit your work, change your work or employer. Changing your role in the same company may help you to regain your energy as you fulfill your passion. But remember to stay in control of your situation. Drop your anchor awhile. Review what you can control and what you can't, as demonstrated in the Life Control Model.

Change may occur quickly, but that doesn't mean that we have to take immediate action without giving the changes significant thought. Changing conditions, and maybe the economic environment, challenge our strategies all the time. Sometimes it's an internal change; at times an external force threatens our strategic success. Long-term goals can be clouded as we accommodate actions for short-term gains. Think about sailing our boat. As the weather, wind, or conditions change, we adjust our sails and tack to continue in our intended direction, using short-term adjustments to navigate to our desired destination, or long-term goal.

Future American business practices need to be more in tune with the way change occurs. As we've discussed, changes are occurring in a faster cycle all the time and the rate of change in the global economy will continue to increase. The demands for business to change products, technology, distribution methods, and customer care must advance or the company will become stagnant and eventually be bought out or die. At this time Toyota is the largest producer of vehicles in the world. They've met the challenges of change and customer needs for more than thirty-five years. Toyota created a unique culture in order for the company to advance the way it has. American car makers have not been able to duplicate the Toyota culture: now they are in crisis. Other car manufacturers are now gaining on Toyota, especially after the large number of recalls they experienced in 2010. Honda, Hyundai, and Ford sales are up because of the recalls. Toyota may not be able to ever recapture their previous market share. They must continue to change to be successful.

Mastering changes in organizations is a constant learning process. The most successful companies engage individual associates quickly, train them for new functions, and allow them to think and act in a manner that is almost self-managing. The leaders of such businesses stand by to support the person doing the work and provide the resources to get the job done and fulfill the mission. American executives don't seem to slow down sufficiently in order to invest up-front time during a new initiative in order to start it on a solid foundation of understanding, engagement, and mutual learning.

— *Communicating Change Efforts in the Business*

Communicating changes may seem simple at first, but the way we communicate changes to others is most important. Of course, we want to be clear, logical, and persuasive. It takes more effort than planning a speech. People want to know what the changes will impact. They want to know what this new initiative will look like in the future. They will have many questions as time goes on.

Communicating the desired changes doesn't always get the message across. First, people receive information differently. This means that leaders must communicate the messages five or six different ways: in writing via e-mail and memos, verbally, graphically, etc. Associates need to have their questions answered in order to help them understand and process what they need to do to satisfy their questions so they can get down to business. And as leaders, we need to understand the people we lead. We shouldn't make assumptions about how they will respond. We need to talk with them, share information, and listen to what they think and how they feel about the changes. It's simply a matter of respect. If we don't slow down and have these conversations, we may get a weak response or minimal buy-in. Associate resistance is counterproductive in the long run. Leaders want individuals to take the initiative to make the changes happen. But it's up to the leader to make sure that the associate is clearly engaged, for personal as well as professional reasons.

At times, leaders at all levels need to help people change in order to meet the challenges or demands of the revised mission, project, or initiative. Managers need to focus on individuals if the changes are to be implemented successfully. Skills may need updating. Training for new technology may be necessary. But most of the time, managers will focus on what is happening to the individuals. How can each person accept the changes and then support them over time? My experience has demonstrated that in an organization, "change happens one person at a time." Leaders can not effectively command change to occur. They must instead talk and listen and coach the individuals who are impacted. Of course, they usually need other managers and supervisors to help them in this coaching process. Tom DeMarco[33] says that, "The key role of middle management is reinvention … the distinction between companies that survive the turmoil of our changing economies and those that don't is middle management in its change agent role." I know from personal experience that individual care and attention are the fastest and most effective ways to get buy-in and support the emotional changes.

---

33 DeMarco, Tom, *Slack, Getting Past Burnout, Busywork and the Myth of Total Efficiency.*

– *It's Personal*

Successful managers lead change on a personal level. We all deal with changes differently. We may all be in a different place in our individual cycles of change. We probably feel uncomfortable with the changes, and we need to know that our world may be better if we accept those changes. Business leaders are asking us to do more with less, especially during financial crises. They need to discuss the reasons for asking people to do more on a personal level. "My manager needs to slow down and help me understand how these actions or changes will benefit me as well as the business." Remember: "What's in it for me?" Each person needs to personally see and understand the benefits or drawbacks to them. Dialogue must occur. Talking with every individual will help each person process the information, create mental pictures of the outcomes, and define the personal changes necessary in order for them to buy into the efforts. There is no magic solution to getting people to change. There is no cadence. Everyone makes their choices to accept or reject at their own pace. If there is any magic to this communications process, then the magic in the dialogue.

Coaching others is the way to help them process and create their own personal map of the journey that the manager has described. Letting people talk helps them think. They want to have a "voice." They are able to discover opportunities they may have never thought about in the past if they can take the time to process the change and see the possibilities. We all need to get beyond the personal angst and start thinking of the possibilities during this change effort. The new initiative may be a great opportunity, but it may take individuals some time to process and move beyond the emotional barriers. Even if managers spell out what they think are the opportunities, the associates need to think it through before adopting the manager's opinions. Make time to help the people you work with to process and buy into the rationale for the changes. This will make a big difference in the speed of implementing the changes.

Businesses usually have long-term plans and annual strategic plans. They also have a budget cycle that must be coordinated with the strategy, for many reasons. Businesses may be missing a valuable step in their business planning that you have taken in your personal life. Fredric Hudson saw an opportunity over twenty years ago for a business to renew itself in a manner similar to a personal renewal process. I believe that businesses should renew themselves once a year, just as each of us should.

— *Align Intellect, Emotions, and Intuition*

A good question to ask at this time is, "How do I manage the intellectual awareness *and* the emotions related to the changes I know need to be made?" Our minds seem to figure out what needs to be done in a logical manner, but our emotions can be in conflict with our mind. This isn't uncommon. Our emotions need to catch up with our intellectual logic, and at times our logic needs to catch up with our emotions. Emotions are fundamental to intuition. My unscientific conclusion is that emotions and intuition are connected. It's important that we recognize the difference in order to understand what's going on. We must slow down and have patience with any internal conflict that may occur and recognize it for what it is. What is real? What values are in conflict? What's really important to me? What is my best response? What choices do I have? These are question that may surface while you are sorting out intellectual logic, emotions, and intuition. Give yourself some time. Just keep the conflict in front of you as something that needs to be resolved. Your patience will pay off in making the right choice.

— *Renew Commitments*

Firm agreements need to be made between you and your spouse and/or family members. An agreement is a commitment that comes out of a plan that is designed with your family. Ask your spouse to keep you honest about keeping these agreements. You will make choices daily about whether you keep or break these agreements. It's easy to drift away from promises. Stay conscious of your agreements. You can rationalize your way into dangerous territory, and rationalization can lead to many broken promises. It's easier to break promises to close family members than it is to people outside the family. Families most often forgive us. Broken commitments in the work environment have serious professional consequences. Broken commitments with the family eventually create strained relations.

– *Depend on Values*

Your values are your anchor and inspiration. You can always depend on them. You have defined your current purpose based on your values and character. Be confident; make the right choices to modify your plan because they are based on your values. Confidence attracts the courage to do the right things and make the best possible choices. If you practice this type of decision making, your intellectual and intuitive natures will be aligned. Then, the choices related to the changes you want to make will become clearer. You can then direct your energy in a positive and confident direction and take action.

> *"When your work is aligned with your values, you tap into the 'fire within'. The highest achievements of people and organizations arise when people feel inspired to accomplish something that fits their top values." – Anne Greenblatt, Stanford University*[34]

Be Proactive

I an earlier chapter we discussed making adjustments in your current chapter of your life: a cycle within a cycle. Something has occurred that indicates that you need to change something or take care of something short-term. This second cycle will not interfere with the place you are in now; you will intervene in your own chapter to take control and make some adjustments. You have recognized that what is happening may jeopardize your purpose plan.

Take a five-thousand-foot view of the impact and pressures placed upon you. Look at the "forest." You can only do this if you slow down, step out of the daily routine, and think bigger. You can make the choice to sidestep the impact and take advantage of the changes in order to advance your purpose or mission. But if you're so busy trying to keep up the pace, you won't see the opportunities or possibilities. Think ahead. Create possible scenarios, and see how your purpose fits into each scenario. Then you are more likely to stay in control, maintain your purpose, and make the necessary adjustments to your plan. Of course, if a new chapter

---

34 Sherren, Joseph, "Ethics in the Workplace." *Summit*, Canada's magazine on public sector purchasing, June 2005, page 1.

of your life and work is on the horizon it may be the time to renew your purpose.

Maintaining the Plan

I suggest that we renew our chapter in our lives once a year. External forces beyond our control may cause us to make significant changes sooner. Renewing ourselves means merely updating our plan. I have been in my chapter for six years without making a significant change. I manage my own consulting business, so I have a great deal of control. I have renewed the way I approach my business annually. I have changed my business model three times over ten years. Associates in my group have changed over the years. I have also added new services to my business: Next New Adventure (retirement coaching), group coaching within one company, and Coach Right Now, training leaders to use coaching skills.

Slowing down periodically to have a discussion with your spouse or friend about what's going on and why you are doing what you are doing is a maintenance activity that's important to sustaining the vision and activities in your plan.

Are your activities putting meaning in your family life?

Where is the energy being placed?

Are you staying centered in the intended direction?

These questions, and the conversations you have, center you in the ultimate direction: your purposes. Force the dialogue at times, but make sure you talk about what is important to each individual as the individual relates to the purpose of the *family*. Help others refocus on what the family wanted to accomplish. Be in touch with how conditions and needs have changed. It will be the judgment of your spouse and you as to whether it is appropriate to adjust the family plans to adapt to current changing conditions. Be cautious that you don't sacrifice any of the basic family values that you hold dear. These discussion practices are equally important in a single-parent home.

Make an annual trek somewhere just to revisit and renew your purpose plan. Don't get too comfortable or life will swiftly pass without your noticing what is happening to you or whether you are still on track with your purpose plans or mission at work. Remember "Bud's Law": nothing really changes unless you get uncomfortable. Get some feedback on how you're doing; understand the changes occurring and how you should adjust to those changes.

My wife and I realized that the house we built and made improvements on was becoming too big for us and our lifestyle. We were also thinking about a summer home on a lake that could ultimately become our permanent home. We ended up choosing a smaller new home close to where we lived. We put a down payment on the house and signed a contract. That night I looked at my nervous wife and said, "It's time we move on." It wasn't a dramatic move for us; we had moved to Singapore at one time, but it was dramatic to a number of people. "You have a beautiful home, why do you want to move?" "We'll miss you as a neighbor, why do you want to do this?" "What has changed to make you move away from us?" Our grown children even said, "If you move to a smaller house, we won't have any place to sleep when we visit you three or four times a year."

We realized that other people didn't want us to change our lives. In their friendly and caring way, they wanted to influence some control over us. It's also interesting how we behaved in response to how others want us to behave so that they could remain comfortable. Interestingly, some of our friends started to renew their plans because of our actions. Some of our friends updated their homes after we did and decided to sell their houses. I guess we triggered some need inside them to move on in their own way.

The Questions You Ask

Renewal is a process of questioning your direction; the chapter you are in, the actions you are taking, and if you need to change anything in your life. It may seem as though you are turning things upside down. You are merely facing reality and asking some important questions. Be bold. This may call for some minor adjustments—or maybe more dramatic ones.

Figuring It Out

Regardless of whether you're forced to reassess your situation because of change or are proactively assessing where you are, this is the recommended process.

Take a look at where you are in your cycle of change. How would you describe the phase of your cycle as it relates to your purpose plan? If I ask you the following questions, what are your responses?

- What do you think and feel about how you are going about moving forward?
- Are you still doing what you are passionate about?
- What are you learning that will get you ready for the next moves?
- Are you strengthening or building relationships that are important in your life?
- What adjustments to your plans should you make, if any?
- And, most importantly, what do you *really* want?

Your responses will help you become aware of where you are as it relates to where you want to be. This is living your life intentionally. Slow down to check in with your plans, or else you may lose traction and just wander around.

Time to Pause

What new approaches will you take to making meaningful changes?

Describe events beyond your control that may impact your plan over the next twelve months.

11
Maintain Your Joy

You have described what success is for you for this chapter of your life. You developed a plan in order to have meaning in your life and work. Pursuing this plan will create joy in your life.

I think happiness is a feeling that comes and goes and is present for a short period of time. I haven't met anyone yet who is always happy. Joy is more of a constant or growing feeling that lasts over a long period of time. Joy endures. I want to distinguish between them for the purpose of what I want to discuss in this chapter.

Use Check-in Questions

As you pursue your plan, periodically check in to see how you feel about your progress. Ask yourself questions such as:

- Am I content with my direction?
- Am I accomplishing what I really want for myself?
- Am I still values-based in my actions and activities?
- Am I standing up for what I believe?
- Am I still living my life with intention?

Keep these questions handy, maybe on a three-by-five card. Your responses will be short: yes or no. Reflecting on these check-in questions will not only keep you focused but will start a healthy dialogue with yourself or a trusted friend. While your responses are short, the thoughts around the questions may provide insight.

In the past I met every two months with the members of my consulting and coaching group. Someone always offered a check-in question for us to think about; and we shared our thoughts with each other. At times, we spent an entire hour discussing new beliefs and discoveries. The practice grounded and energized us; we responded to the questions that we all processed separately and shared and learned from the dialogue we engaged in together.

Stimulate yourself with challenging check-in questions. You may discover how to overcome a barrier that you have encountered. You may experience breakthroughs. You will also recognize when you are on track with your plan, experiencing the joy of progressing toward your mission and goals.

Solicit Feedback

Periodically assessing where we are can be accomplished in other ways. We can seek out a coach to help us stay centered on our journey or make some adjustments to the "how" of where we want to go. We can seek help through reading material on the Internet and in books that will also stimulate questions and answers. We want some feedback once in awhile. Don't we want feedback from our boss or people we work with? Feedback also needs to be solicited periodically. We should make it a habit. Keep in mind that we are all working on something. So the question "How am I doing?" isn't intimidating at all. We frequently think that we are taking risks, or we think others will think we are paranoid. Get over it. People respect the coworkers who want to improve and grow and request feedback. It does not mean you are insecure. You are only expressing the desire to keep learning to improve.

Locate a Helpful Mentor

Not all of us have a mentor, but mentors are frequently great sources of feedback and suggestions on how to move ahead. Check in with your mentors if you have them. They may want to help you. We should find people who know what our passions are. They know our plan and purpose. They have probably helped us build our plan. At times we change mentors because they may have different experiences and knowledge that will help us at different stages of our development. Trusted individuals will ask us insightful questions to help us process and think.

Measure Your Progress

Measuring the progress of the change process is important in order to see a return on your efforts. You need to know that you are getting traction. You need to also celebrate early successes to reinforce your actions and gain momentum. Measures are important in order to be alert to drifting away from the purpose or mission objectives. We all need emotional satisfaction from our sweat and pain. We also may need to make some adjustments, as we've already discussed.

On a personal level, we know that we will work on our purpose through this cycle of change for as long as it takes in order to achieve our goals. The models, plans, and measures are the framework for the changes we are driving. They give us context as well as structure. You and I are at the helm of our sailboats. We must make choices about how we will reach our destinations. We depend on our navigation charts and compass. It's rarely smooth sailing. Stay in control, and keep moving forward.

Designing and following a model is an effective way to guide you and measure your progress. You can use existing models that were discussed in pervious chapters; i.e. Cycle of Renewal, the Life Control Model. If you design your own model, you are more likely to use it more because you own it. Any model you choose will help you assess where you are currently, where you should move next, and what adjustments you may need to make.

Your written purpose plan—or any action plan—will also measure your progress; an action plan details what you plan to do and when you expect to take action. You usually identify milestones to benchmark progress. Ask yourself, "Am I satisfied with my progress?" If you're not satisfied, change what you've been doing and move on. Don't spend too much time in the past; just keep moving forward.

Locate a Coach

Talk with a coach about your purpose, plan, and progress. This will help process your thoughts and get you unstuck as you develop a plan to move forward. Even though you are well on your way and focusing on your purpose or mission, anyone can get "blown off course" within a chapter of their life. Talk with an objective person whom you trust and who will listen to you. Professional coaches are available to get you back on course, help you make appropriate adjustments to your plan, and assist you in continuing to move forward. Consultant coaches can also help renew your business and move it in new directions.

Professional help gets you where you want to go faster than if you struggle through it alone. The coach will review your plan for awareness and progress on an ongoing basis. The coach also has you check to see if something has changed in order to suggest a shift in your plans. Coaches hold you accountable and help remove the barriers you face in making progress. They are reflective and assist you in processing how you will face your challenges. When searching for the right coach, make sure that he or she has professional credentials from the International Coach Federation or other credible associations that monitor coaching standards. This credential means they have training and experience to be a professional coach.

I want to mention an important caution when seeking help. Family members are not as helpful as coaches or mentors. Families are biased. It's difficult for them to be objective. Even as a professionally trained coach, I don't coach my family. Periodically, I can share what I know, but coaching doesn't have much affect on them.

Avoid Excuses and Laziness

Exercising to keep our bodies strong is hard work but must be done for healthy living. Being lazy keeps us from exercising. Excuses are a form of laziness. Procrastination doesn't take us anywhere either. The longer we make excuses the longer it takes to meet our objectives. Our purpose plan details the important actions we want to take in our life. I encounter clients who say they haven't reviewed their purpose plan because they've been too busy. An excuse for busyness isn't allowed when I am coaching a client!

Type "A" people rarely admit that they are lazy, because they are energetic in some areas of their life and work but not in other areas. We can be energetic and passionate about our work but lazy about spending time with our family or talking with our spouse or even taking care of ourselves. Be cautious about your laziness. We all have areas of laziness. You don't have to be a "couch potato" to be lazy. Ask yourself, "What important things are not getting my attention?" This question slows you down. When you are into busyness you don't slow down to ask and respond to these questions.

Meaningful activities are what we want to focus on. Our purpose plan provides the clear direction we want in the present chapter of our life. Ultimately, we are seeking joy. Joy is the result of having meaning in our life. Life without meaning is empty and frequently leads to busyness or just emptiness. If you don't know where you are going, any destination will do. "Get real" by slowing down and confronting your issues and designing the life you want. Be at the top of your game by making life a meaningful effort. Work hard at the things in your life that are important. Your passions will come alive.

Sustain Your Purpose

As I mentioned previously, I am still in the chapter of my life that I designed for myself years ago. I've made some adjustments to my action plan, but I still have the essence of my purpose firmly in my grasp and the meaning of how I live and work. I'm in control of what I can control. Spending the time on identifying my purpose is something I should have done twenty years earlier. I wasn't slowing down long enough at that time to plan my life and work around my strengths, desires, and enthusiasms to help individuals and businesses grow. My purpose is now to help people and businesses discover their potential, build a plan, and execute the plan with passion. I am very happy today and living my purpose intentionally. You have the opportunity to slow down and to look and listen to what's in your heart and plan around the desires, hopes, and abilities that serve you and others.

Having a clear purpose is having a solid foundation that supports your decisions and choices. Staying balanced may be difficult at times, but balance is what is most desirable. Continuously centering on purpose and the most important people in your life provides stability and confidence. Staying grounded in values and purpose maintains the balance. Slowing down to think about what you value is key to looking at reality; center to focus on what is important to you, question the pressures at hand, and take action by making a choice.

Sustainability is very important to corporate executives, managers, and coaches. Even though we have removed the barriers, adjusted our plans, and renewed ourselves from time to time, sustainability is always a challenge. We can't get lazy. We need to refresh ourselves and make meaningful changes in what we want in our lives. Businesses want to get a return on their investment of time, energy, and resources. We want that for our personal life as well.

How do we sustain our purpose and passions? It's a matter of focusing on our higher purpose, whether it is God's purpose for us or the highest purpose that we have described for us personally. We can design many different chapters in our lives throughout a lifetime and pursue our ultimate purpose or higher purpose simultaneously. Redefining or reinventing ourselves doesn't mean we need to change our highest level of purpose.

Our highest level of purpose also helps to sustain us. Many times in business a high-level vision provides an ultimate achievement. Make sure that the adjustments in your plans remain in alignment with your ultimate mission or purpose. Periodically refresh your visual image while maintaining the purpose in the context of your vision. Refresh yourself as the world and environment changes. Renew you life while maintaining the integrity of your ultimate purpose. I believe that we must keep growing in our purpose until we die.

We are pursuing joy and happiness throughout our lives. Let other things come into your life that will enhance or accelerate your pursuit of dreams and mission. Live your life to the fullest every day. You are the only one who can make the important choices to bring true joy and happiness into your life.

I hope you have accepted the importance of slowing down in order to be more productive in your personal and professional life. Slowing down has provided me with a great and powerful perspective. I've done this for myself, and I've done this for my clients. I wish you well on your journey.

Make it meaningful. You will find true joy. Share your experience and knowledge with others. Sharing knowledge is powerful!

Rough Seas to Smooth Sailing

Today, as my wife and I were walking at a new recreation center in our town, we both noticed a woman wearing a t-shirt that said, "Got purpose?" similar to the magazine ad that asks, "Got milk?" I suggest that as milk was essential early in our life when we were growing up, purpose is essential in order to grow as adults and find long-term joy.

Purpose is the driver behind your success. These successes are linked to long-term satisfaction. Frequently we sacrifice or work hard at our short-term objectives because they lead us to fulfilling our mission. Listen to your feelings as you move through these short-term activities and objectives. If everything seems to be great, push on to the next objectives and actions.

As we visit a renewal process over and over again during our lifetime, short-term happiness will become long-term joy and success. Through the ups and downs of our journey we will find the joy we seek when we live our lives intentionally and with purpose.

I hope you have read this book slowly enough to experience the power of the exercises, completing them as you moved along. I want to suggest that you read through this book in another year from now. I hope these thoughts continue to enrich your life and the lives of those you love and meet.

I wish you smooth sailing as you tack your way to your destinations throughout your life.

Time to Pause

Write a higher-level purpose statement that summarizes your detailed plan.

Write out a timeline about when you will periodically review your purpose plan.

Now place the dates on your calendar.

About the Author

Bud Roth is a seasoned executive with over twenty-five years' experience working with Fortune 500 companies. He has in-depth experience in change management, organizational development, selecting and developing good talent, and international expatriate management. Bud's corporate background includes financial services, manufacturing, consumer products, and information technology. He has successfully coached executives and senior managers from small businesses to large corporations.

Bud has worked in a wide variety of corporate environments, including a three-year assignment in Singapore. He has worked through mergers, fast-changing business conditions, and survival strategies. Bud renewed organizations to meet current business conditions. His organizational development strategies have been applied to help corporations succeed over the long term. He has also developed a coaching and consulting process to support expatriates on assignment and those returning from foreign assignments. He brings creative solutions that impact each unique business situation.

Bud started his own consulting business, Roth Consulting Group (RCG), in 2000. RCG focuses on consulting in strategic planning, organizational renewal, team development, and executive coaching. Bud is in contact with a cadre of seasoned consultants and coaches throughout the United States. RCG has implemented results-oriented coaching environments, improved individual and business performance, and helped executives balance their personal lives while improving their leadership effectiveness.

Bud has seven years of sales experience and an extensive track record in training and development. He has demonstrated his abilities in process improvement, managing organizational change, and developing "vision-to-action" planning from first-line leaders to corporate level executives.

Bud has a BA in business from Carthage College and obtained his professional coaching certification from the Hudson Institute of Coaching in Santa Barbara, CA. He received the professional certified coach credential from the International Coach Federation. He is also certified in preretirement coaching, which he describes as "Your Next Adventure."

Bud lives in Carmel, Indiana, with his wife, Cathy. They have three grown children and seven grandchildren.

Please contact Bud at budroth@rothcg.com for more information or for consulting, coaching, and speaking engagements.

For more information about this book and Bud's blogs go to *bemoreproductive-slowdown.com* Also follow Bud on Twitter.

Appendix

Part I
Living Life Out of Control
1. The Fast Changing World: Living Without Purpose

Time to Pause Exercise
- Name three of your biggest time wasters.

- What can you stop doing?

- What short-term activities are you pursuing that have little effect on long-term goals?

- What actions will you take?

2. Static Survival: Living Without Growth

Time to Pause Exercise
- What stories are you holding that you need to clear up to discover if they are the truth?

- Describe the new stories about how you will live your life and work.

- Listen and then confront fears and beliefs that are barriers to you moving ahead.

165

Part II
Regaining Control
3. Models for Managing Change

Time to Pause Exercise
- Design a model for your life based on where you want to go and your purpose.

- Establish milestones for measuring your progress to achieve your goals.

4. The Life Control Model™: What You Can Control and What You Can't

Time to Pause Exercise
- Review the Life Control Model sailboat. Assess how you are responding to what is out of your control. Then, identify what is in your control that you previously thought was beyond your control.

- What do you need to investigate first in order to make a course change in your life and work?

- What preparations do you need to make before you move on to adjusting your direction?

- List three actions you will take to get back on course toward your destination.

5. Slow Down To Be More Productive

Time to Pause Exercise
Try these exercises to measure you productivity.
- Take time to think about how you can be more productive by controlling your work environment. Ask yourself about the time you waste. It's really in your control to manage this important issue.

- Take the opportunity to make some changes in the way you work. Answer the question, "What am I doing that wastes time?"

- Spend the next two weeks recording the work you are doing hour by hour. Develop a spreadsheet that you can complete as the day progresses. Review what you've worked on in the morning before lunch. Repeat the review at the end of the day. At the end of two weeks, summarize what you have worked on as a percentage of your day. Identify the wasted or unproductive time. Later, decide if the work you have completed made any difference to the goals of your department or business. Don't perform this exercise longer than two weeks. This time period will provide the information you need to make significant changes. These exercises are laborious, but stick with it. Now, make adjustments. Stop doing some things. Discuss areas of waste and value with your boss and coworkers. Choose to do the work that adds value and supports the current mission.

- Contrast your busiest days with the days you feel you accomplish the most. What was the difference in the way you were working?

- Contrast how you felt about what you accomplished last Saturday, doing your errands, and what you accomplished last Friday with the pressures at work.

- What work habits can you control and change to make your day more productive, less stressful?

6. Slow Down for Your Well-Being

Time to Pause Exercise
- What are the three things you want to do to be in better shape and take care of yourself?

- What spiritual needs are missing in your life?

- While reviewing your priorities, what two or three things can you let go of and not do?

- What is the most important issue you need to face and push back on?

- Talk with each member of your family alone. Ask your questions and answer theirs.

Part III
Planning Purpose and Action
7. Rediscover Who You Are

Time to Pause Exercise
- Describe five strengths that you can develop to the next level.

- Seek situations where you made a good decision by integrating your brain power, heart, and intuition. Now use these elements to decide about something in your future.

- Tonight, with your spouse, family member, or friend, ask a thought-provoking, open-ended question and then listen to what they say for a deeper meaning. Be very quiet and don't interrupt. Use your intuition to form other questions to get to the essence of the response. Articulate your discovery.

- Consider a situation you are currently struggling with. What are your feelings about the situation, and how does this impact you? *First*, use your intuition to find a response. *Then*, look at the facts. Test your responses with someone else.

8. How to Plan

Time to Pause Exercise
- Review, complete, and adjust your written plan for the next chapter of your life.

- Plan your technical and organization needs.

Part IV
Maintaining Purpose and Progress
9. Stick to Your Plan

Time to Pause Exercise

- What events frequently reoccur that distract you from pursuing your mission, purpose or priorities?

- What will you do to stop or control the distractions?

- Review the technical devices you are currently using.

- Are the devices serving you in completing your mission?

- What technology or maintenance is hindering your work?

- Name three actions you can take to get more control over the devices and your time.

- When will you change how you operate? Get moving!

10. Reassess Your Plan

Time to Pause Exercise

- What new approaches will you take to making meaningful changes?

- Describe events out of your control that may impact your plan over the next twelve months.

11. Maintain Your Joy

Time to Pause Exercise

- Write a higher-level purpose statement that summarizes your detailed plan.

- Write out a timeline for when you will periodically review your purpose plan.

- Now, place the dates on your calendar.

Bibliography

Ballantyne, Robert J., "Decisions Using Intuition and Creativity," An essay unpublished, July 3, 1996, http:/www.ballantyne.com/Intuition.html

Bridges, William, "Making the Most of Change," *Managing Transitions*, Addison-Wesley Publishing Company, 1991.

Buckingham, Marcus and Clifton, Donald O., PhD, *Now Develop Your Strengths, The revolutionary program that shows you how to develop your unique talents and strengths—and those of the people you manage*, 1st edition. Based on the Gallup study of over two million people. Free Press: 2001.

Buettner, Dan, "Find Purpose, Live Longer," Mind and Body, *AARP The Magazine*, November & December 2008, page 32.

Claudia Wallis, "The Multitasking Generation," *Time*, March 19, 2006.

Covey, Stephen R., Merrill, A. Roger, Merrill, Rebecca R., *First Things First*, Simon and Schuster, 1994.

DeMarco, Tom, *Slack, Getting Past Burnout, Busywork, and the Myth of Total Efficiency*, Broadway Books, New York, 2001.

"Don't Multitask—Your Brain Will Thank You", "Get More Done", Issie Lapowsky, Inc., April, 2013, page 66

"Drop that Blackberry! Multitasking may be harmful." *Health Magazine*, 2009, http://www.cnn.com/2009/HEALTH/08/25/multitasking. harmful/index.html.

Funk and Wagnalls, *The Readers Digest Great Encyclopedia Dictionary*, Standard College Dictionary, 1968.

Goleman, Daniel and Boyatzis, Richard, "Social Intelligence and the Biology of Leadership," *Harvard Business Review*, September 2008.

Hudson, Fredric M., PhD, *The Handbook of Coaching, A Comprehensive Resource Guide for Managers, Executives, Consultants, and Human Resource Professionals*, Jossey-Bass Publishers, San Fransisco, 1999.

Kotter, John, *Leading Change*, Harvard Business School Press, 1996.

Leider, Richard J., *The Power of Purpose*, Barrett-Koehler Publishing, Inc., 1997.

Lohr, Steve, "Slow Down Brave Multitasker and Don't Read This in Traffic," *New York Times*, quoting the Institute for the Future of the Mind at Oxford University, March 26, 2007.

Nilsson, Gunnar, *Human Bandwidth*, Rapid Creek Publishing, 2002.

O'Neil, John, *The Paradox of Success*, Jeremy P. Tracher/Putnum, member of Penguin Putnam, Inc., 1993.

Patterson, Kerry, McMillan, Ron, Grenny, Joseph and Switzler, Al, *Crucial Conversations, Tools for Talking When Stakes are High*, McGraw-Hill, 2002.

Peale, Norman Vincent, *How to Make Positive Imaging Work for You*, originally published by Fleming H. Revell Company, 1982. Formerly published under the title *Dynamic Imaging and Positive Imaging*, page 5.

Pearsall, Paul, PhD, *Toxic Success, How to Stop Striving and Start Thriving*, Ocean Publishing, Inc., 2002.

Sherren, Joseph, "Ethics in the Workplace," *Summit*, Canada's magazine on public sector purchasing, June 2005, page 1.

Spherion and Harris Interactive study, 1997, Chapter 6, page 11.

Success Factors Web site, "Performance and Talent Management Trends Survey," 2007, http://www.successfactors.com/articles/performance-management-trends/2007.

"The Multi-tasking Generation," "Why Homework?" A blog, Time.com.

"The Power of Thoughts," http://www.abundance-and-happiness.com.

Ulrich, David and Wendy, *The Why of Work, How Great Leaders Build Abundant Organizations That Win*, McGraw Hill, 2010.

Yankelovich, Daniel, *The Magic of Dialogue, Transforming Dialogue into Cooperation*, First Touchstone, 2001.